Managerial Communication Strategies: An Applied Casebook

Annette M. Veech, Ph.D.

John M. Olin School of Business
Washington University

Upper Saddle River, New Jersey 07458

Library of Congress Cataloging-in-Publication Data

Veech, Annette M.
    Managerial communication strategies : an applied casebook / by Annette M.
Veech.
      p. cm.
    Includes bibliographical references and index.
    ISBN 0-13-060821-1
    1. Communication in management—Case studies. 2. Business communication—Case
studies I. Title.
    HD30.3 V44   2001
    658.4'5—dc21   2001036022

Acquisitions Editor: David Parker
Editor-in-Chief: Jeff Shelstad
Assistant Editor: Jennifer Surich
Editorial Assistant: Virginia Sheridan
Media Project Manager: Michele Faranda
Senior Marketing Manager: Debbie Clare
Marketing Assistant: Brian Rappelfeld
Managing Editor: John Roberts
Production Coordinator: Kelly Warsak
Permissions Coordinator: Suzanne Grappi
Associate Director, Manufacturing: Vincent Scelta
Production Manager: Arnold Vila
Manufacturing Buyer: Diane Peirano
Cover Designer: Bruce Kenselaar
Composition: BookMasters, Inc.
Full-Service Project Management: BookMasters, Inc.
Printer/Binder: Victor Graphics
Cover Printer: Victor Graphics

Pearson Education LTD.
Pearson Education Australia PTY, Limited
Pearson Education Singapore, Pte. Ltd
Pearson Education North Asia Ltd
Pearson Education, Canada, Ltd
Pearson Educación de Mexico, S.A. de C.V.
Pearson Education–Japan
Pearson Education Malaysia, Pte. Ltd

10 9 8 7 6 5 4 3 2 1
ISBN 0-13-060821-1

This book is dedicated to people willing to pursue creative thought and positive team spirit.

Contents

Preface

First, let me explain how to differentiate this casebook from others in the arena of business and managerial communications. Many fine textbooks focus on specific business writing and presentation skills; those textbooks delve into areas of expertise such as rules of grammar and the tactical techniques necessary to build effective presentations. Writing and presentation skills are overviewed in this casebook because I believe that those skills are necessary prerequisites in managerial communications. This casebook, however, clearly does not compete with textbooks specifically designed to help professors teach business communication skills, but does serve as a complement to those textbooks.

Next, I must share my personal bias regarding effective managerial communication. I believe that a successful communicator/manager possesses two dimensions of skills: What I label the *science* and the *art* of communicating.

The first dimension, the *science* of effective communication, comprises such foundation skills as writing and speaking effectively, adhering to organizational style guidelines, staying on point (i.e., maintaining the central idea of a message), and succinctly delivering consistent messages. These foundation skills, the science, help formulate our perceptions of a manager's personal integrity and credibility.

The second dimension, the art of effective communication, incorporates such advanced and sometimes intuitive skills as reading the audience, separating facts from emotions, varying persuasive strategies to match others' personal styles, and applying group facilitation methods to solve team problems and identify the root causes of business issues. These skills, the art, lead to our perceptions regarding the extent to which we trust a manager.

I believe that competent managers excel in the science of effective communication. Through empirical evidence, I have come to believe that stellar managers excel in the science and the art of effective communication. Stellar managers consistently communicate effectively as well as mentally strategize in terms of their audience. These managers consider other points of view and seem to intuitively do the right things at the right times for the right people (and people perceive for the right reasons). Stellar managers go beyond doing the right things; stellar managers do things right.

These points lead me to explain why I organized this casebook around functional areas. Managers may have originally trained in a specific field (e.g., finance or marketing), but managers eventually must demonstrate some level of expertise across many fields (e.g., finance, marketing, human resources, and operations). The functional tasks, however, recur on a daily basis. Therefore, I organized the casebook around critical functions to mirror the daily life of any manager.

Finally, some readers of more traditional business and managerial communications textbooks may feel that the clustering of cases is rather disparate. I defend this by saying that no manager has the luxury of responding to neat and tidy situations. The reality of a manager's life is that anything can happen, and unfortunately, often does. Therefore, my intent in gathering a range of cases is to present people with a continuum of realistic situations, based on composite facts—and my intent is to help managers think creatively and quickly.

I hope that this casebook helps managers and students of management capitalize on what they may already know (e.g., running brainstorms), creatively apply accepted business tools (e.g., SWOT Analysis) to what they perceive as communications issues, and consequently accomplish better results—with tasks *and* people. A manager perceived by colleagues as effective is probably viewed as a person with personal integrity and credibility, and, therefore, a manager whom people trust.

Acknowledgments

I wish to thank the following reviewers for their input:

Dr. John Penrose, San Diego State University
Mohamed Zainuba, Texas Southern University
Christine Kelly, New York University
Teresa Parkey Barao, University of Maryland
Dr. Joan Rivera, Angelo State University
Dr. Lucinda Sinclair, Longwood College
Marianna Larsen, Utah State University
Linda Hall, South Plains College
Dr. Doug Andrews, University of Southern California

How to Use this Book

Purpose

This casebook is designed as a supplemental text to primary communication textbooks in university courses, workshops, and individual learning endeavors. The cases allow readers to analyze, draw conclusions, and recommend solutions.

A three-step problem-solving methodology is recommended in the casebook. In real life, every case is different; the people involved make judgment calls based on unique organizational and interpersonal contexts.

Therefore, any strategy in the casebook is not intended as the sole solution. Class discussions and the experiences of individuals lead to suggestions of numerous strategies. The ultimate benefit of the case approach is that someone always has a fresh idea.

How to Work Through the Cases

Cases are based on composite facts. When individuals were interviewed, their real names and quotes were noted.

Use three steps to work through each case:

Step #1: Review the Big Picture
Step #2: Analyze the Facts and Emotions (F&Es)
Step #3: Design the Strategy.

Note to Individual Readers

If you peruse the book on your own, read through the three steps of each case in sequence. You will see tools and techniques that you may readily apply in your communication efforts.

Note to Classroom Instructors

If you use the book as a supplement to your course:

1. Give your students copies of Step #1: Review the Big Picture for each case.
2. Ask small groups to discuss their ideas for Step #2: Analyze Facts and Emotions (F&Es) and Step #3: Design the Strategy.
3. Follow this with a full group discussion about how students approached the case and why their reasoning led to given strategies.

CHAPTER 1

Manager as Communication Coach

Part One: Present for Impact

*Ask me to listen. But I'm more likely to hear you if you tell me
a persuasive story.*

A Story

"Vita" (not her real name) stands up to deliver a critical sales pitch. She is the manager supervising a capable cross-functional group of energetic people. Her team is pitted against three respected consulting companies; all four teams made the final cut to a

1

"short list." The four consulting teams, in a pre-determined sequence, make their presentations today; Vita's team is third in the lineup. It is 2:00 P.M. and the executives from the client organization are tired: Their minds wander through their ever-accumulating lists of voice mails and e-mails.

Vita's team believes they'll win the project today; their costs are well within acceptable range, they enjoy a solid reputation in the industry, and their project management skills are impeccable.

Vita stands confidently. "Good afternoon, ladies and gentlemen. We are pleased to present our ideas to you this afternoon. We'll spend the next hour talking to you about our project management expertise, our track record in this industry, and our estimated costs and timelines for your project."

In contrast to Vita's belief, her first words could end the competition. Unless a dramatic event occurs (e.g., someone on Vita's team is friends with one of the client executives), Vita's team probably loses this bid before they finish their pitch for the business.

Why? Because Vita and her team forgot about two variables: *point of view* and *attention*. Smart managers focus on point of view and attention as they lead and manage their departments and teams; brilliant managers and salespeople extend that focus to external client relationships. Let's look at point of view first.

Whose Point of View Is Most Important?

Vita's team's point of view was not the most important in this scenario—the client's point of view was the most critical. Vita, as project manager and team leader, didn't realize that what her team sells isn't necessarily what clients buy. Vita tried to sell *expertise and process*; the clients wanted to buy *results for their organization*.

If the client executives weren't already convinced of Vita's team's project management expertise, their track record in the industry, and their realistic project costs and timelines, Vita's team would not have survived the final cut, but Vita missed that point entirely as she delivered the introduction to their sales presentation. Vita introduced her team's presentation by continuing to sell the very features already "conceptually" purchased by the clients. In addition, Vita ignored that, when buried in the mix of four competitive consulting teams, her team's presentation needed to stand apart from the rest in some unique way.

What do the clients really want to hear? They probably want to hear how Vita's team can help them meet *their* objectives—and how Vita's team will do it differently than other consulting teams. At this point, the clients are *curious*: "What can you tell me that I won't hear from your competition?" The clients want to buy *results* like improved sales, enhanced customer satisfaction, and better productivity. The clients only need project management expertise, a solid industry track record, and realistic project costs and timelines to help them reach their desired goals. Vita focused on her *reason for presenting* (i.e., presenters' purpose is "what we have to sell") as opposed to the *clients' reason for listening* (i.e., clients' objectives equate to " what we need").

How Is Attention Won?

The second variable that Vita missed was attention: Why should the executives start to listen to Vita and why should they continue to listen to her team? In other words, why should they care?

Make no mistake. The executives do care. They care about their organization's problems, their shortage of time every single day, and their resource issues. They don't care as much about Vita's *purpose* as Vita believes they do. Why? The answer is simple. The executives know why consulting teams traipse in, one after another: to sell something!

The executives do, however, care about whether Vita's team understands their objectives and needs. They care about hearing something new. And, they care about whether Vita's team *cares enough* about them!

There are two ways to prove all this to restless executives. First, Vita's team must think in terms of the *client's point of view*—they must speak in terms of the *client's objectives*, not the *consulting team's purpose* for speaking. Second, they must grab the *attention*, from the very beginning, of every single executive.

Think about what Vita, in essence, said: "Hi. Our purpose in speaking to you today is . . ." Does this capture the executives' attention from *their* point of view? No. Vita, in reality, gave the clients permission to wander mentally from her presentation before her team even began.

Is There a Solution?

What should Vita have done differently? First, she should have *understood the client's point of view*. If Vita's team had asked themselves six simple questions, they could have identified what the client wants to know:

- What will you do (e.g., can you give me a simple yet elegant solution)?
- Why are you the best (e.g., what makes your team so special)?
- When will you do it (also known as how fast)?
- Where will most of the work occur (e.g., how convenient will it be for me)?
- How much will it cost me (also known as how cheap)?
- Who will help me do it (e.g., will I like working with your team)?

Vita, from word one, should have spoken *for (and from) the client's point of view* to prove that she understood them. If she understood the client's point of view, Vita would first *capture* the executives' attention before she and her team tried to *maintain* it for the next hour. Her introduction (i.e., my purpose for speaking) is the most standard (and perhaps boring) in the history of presentations.

Vita should begin a presentation like this with an unusual introduction, and yet, this is no small task. Vita should have remembered that people are curious. Vita did not capitalize on the fact that *analogies* and *metaphors* pique curiosity and enhance persuasive points. The bottom line is that Vita didn't *tell a story*.

A Story Has a Point of View and a Story Captures Attention

People love stories. Stories coax us to read novels; stories cause us to watch the news; stories even find us looking for happy endings in the stock market reports. There is a story behind everything, and to capture the attention of an audience, we'd better tell a darn good story.

Storytelling is central to the work of many communications companies; clients pay significant sums of money to apply the art of storytelling to their business scenarios. Mr. Peter Giuliano, chairman of Executive Communications Group of Englewood, New

Jersey, was quoted in August 1999 in *The New York Times*: "It requires a high level of strategy. That's what differentiates executive storytelling from telling a story across the kitchen table—the strategic development and intent of the story."

Effective managers understand the value of effective storytelling and they realize that stories accomplish three outcomes with people; stories:

1. Enhance memory
2. Persuade opinions
3. Motivate action

Every manager struggles daily with how best to motivate diverse employees. I ask that you consider the art of the story as one tactic. Let's look at a simple scenario.

You enrolled in an effective presentations class. You participate (even though you don't enjoy delivering presentations) for your own professional and personal reasons: (1) to reduce nervousness before presenting, (2) to speak more effectively, and (3) to persuade employees more efficiently. Your reasons are not exactly the same as the guy or gal sitting next to you in class. Given this scenario, review the following table listing three sample introductions. Which of the introductions in Table 1-1 would you *care* about?

A simple metaphor often paves the way toward a good story because it allows people to visualize their own points of view and because the metaphor captures attention. But as any experienced speaker understands, there is much more to delivering an effective presentation than the introduction.

You Remember What You See

Did you know that the first thing an audience focuses on is *visual*? An audience remembers *what you and your visuals look like* more than they recall *what you've said*. That's a rather scary thought, since we spend so much time deciding what to say to an audience. The truth is, if you and your audiovisuals distract the audience (i.e., if you pace too much, if your slides contain excessive graphics or words), then the audience recalls fewer of your topical points. An audience focuses:

1. First, on the *visual* presentation—you, your visual aids, and basically, anything that moves in the near environment.
2. Second, on *how* you speak—your inflection, pace, tone, and use of pauses.
3. Third, on *what* you say—the words that you think are so important.

Robert A. Brawer, author of *Fictions in Business* and former CEO of Maidenform, tells a story that clearly illustrates our initial focus on the visual. An acquaintance asked Mr. Brawer to have lunch with a Wall Street firm managing partner. Mr. Brawer reluctantly attended; he recounts his memory of that occasion:

> "I remember very little of what he said . . . or about how much money it [the company] had made . . . Strangely enough, what I do remember—and that most vividly—is comparatively insignificant. There was [on the Wall Street partner's shirt] a pair of weighty, elegant cufflinks in hammered gold on meticulously turned, striped French cuffs." (*Fictions in Business*, p. 43)

TABLE 1-1   Sample Presentation Introductions

Sample Introductions	*Why You'd Care (or Wouldn't)*
Sample 1 Good morning. My name is Carl and I'm going to talk to you about how to deliver effective presentations.	Okay, so you wouldn't care about this one much. The speaker using this introduction has only stated the obvious.
Sample 2 "People listen with 25 percent efficiency. Information usually needs to be sent three times to people in order to be received and processed, because people distort 40 to 60 percent of what they hear." That's a quote from Claudyne Wilder, author of a great book entitled *The Presentations Kit* (New York: John Wiley & Sons, Inc., 1994, vii).	You might smirk and say you're reminded of your spouse, children, or a friend. Or you may recall an employee who rarely follows directions correctly. The speaker using this introduction offers people a chance to compare the statistics to their personal experiences.
Sample 3 Have you heard of the Sarah Winchester House in California? The heiress to the Winchester rifle fortune, Sarah, owned the house. Sarah believed that if she constantly remodeled and added on to the house, she'd never die! She hired people to work on that house every day of the week until she, of course, died. The result? A house with stairways leading to brick walls, windows opening into other interior rooms, and a labyrinth of confused rooms and hallways. The house is now open to tours. If you don't have a well-crafted presentation, you may well wind up with a speech like the Sarah Winchester House. Your presentation won't have a clear path from the beginning, the middle, and to the end. Your audience will be confused and perhaps aggravated because they don't know where you're taking them.	Did the story capture your attention? Did it tap into your curiosity about the absurd? Did the metaphor between *house* and *presentation* draw a memorable parallel for you? For many audience members, the answer is "Yes." The speaker using this introduction helps people get caught up in the story so that they create mental visuals of the house. With these visuals in mind, people can more readily envision the need for crafting the foundation of an effective presentation.

Practically speaking, it is not so strange that the foremost item in Mr. Brawer's memory was cuff links, as opposed to the lunch discussion. Managers would do well to remember this when delivering a presentation or coaching their employees: If you're not careful, visual messages overtake the verbal messages.

Let's move from the importance of the visual to how to analyze the *overall context* of a presentation. Table 1-2 outlines tips for understanding your audience and organizing your presentation.

TABLE 1-2 Basic Presentation Strategies	
Analyze	• Your audience, the facilities, the context. Don't underestimate the power of any of these variables.
Identify	• Your purpose: the *what* of your presentation. • Your audience's objective(s): *why* they should listen.
Focus on the Central Idea	• Stated in one memorable phrase or sentence. • To explain the intended benefit(s). • As a "conceptual thread" to integrate all topical points of your presentation.
Create an Interesting Introduction	• To motivate; create interest or curiosity. • That avoids an apology or standard joke. • By starting with a question or quotation. • By using a "dimensional prop." • By clearly stating your central idea. • By previewing the "big picture" of key topical points.
Back up Your Words (Evidence)	• By sharing your personal experiences. • By using analogies or metaphors. • By including the judgment of experts. • By describing examples from other organizations. • By stating statistics or facts.
End with a Powerful Conclusion	• By summarizing key arguments or topical points. • By restating the relevance of your central idea. • By visualizing the benefits. • By urging the audience to take action. • With words like, "in conclusion" or "to summarize" (to ensure that the audience takes note of your final words).
General Tips	• Use the old adage, "Tell them what you're going to tell them; tell them; and, finally, tell them what you told them." • Move from general to specific. • Sequence from large-scale to small-scale ideas. • State the long-term picture and quickly remind the audience of immediate benefits. • Label or enumerate key topical points or sequential steps (to verbally "mark" the listener's place).
Visual Aid Pointers	• People recall more through visual reminders, as opposed to verbal clues only. • Use no more than six (6) bullets on each slide. • Confine a single major idea to one visual slide. • Do not read the slides to your audience; paraphrase and discuss the concepts. • Stand to the left of visuals; don't block any person's view (from any room angle).
Handling Questions & Answers	• Listen to the question; paraphrase so the entire audience hears the question. • If you don't understand the question, ask the person to rephrase. • Ask probing questions when needed.

TABLE 1-2 *(continued)*

- Respond to an "objection" question with a generally acceptable point and then answer (e.g., "While most of us agree that quality has improved; yes, our costs jumped 10 percent."
- With an "objection" question, always state your empathy with their area of concern.
- Give a concise answer, look away from the person who asked the question, and move on to another person's question.
- If you can't handle an issue at the time, write it on a flip chart and tell the audience that you'll get back to them later with the answer.

These basic presentation strategies were probably not all that new for many readers; perhaps they provided a useful reminder, however. Let's now review *five common elements* of effective presentations:

1. Start with an interesting introduction and a memorable central idea.
2. Differentiate your purpose for speaking from the audience's objectives for listening.
3. Explain the big picture of what you are about to say (e.g., similar to a table of contents).
4. Speak in a logical flow and support what you say (i.e., evidence).
5. Conclude powerfully by repeating the central idea and highlighting the benefits.

Tables 1-3, 1-4, and 1-5 are based on the five key elements of effective presentations and provide a structure for evaluating your presentations and formulating basic presentation outlines. Table 1-4 contains the basic script for a brief talk about mistakes made by teams when preparing presentations. The *hunter/farmer* to *explorer/settler* metaphor in the sample originated with a brilliant team of students as they worked with a client in our classroom.

Part Two: Write for Results

Stories are a company's parables of truth. Anecdotal stories are often more powerful than an organization's official written documents.

What You Read Versus What You Believe

Early on, every employee learns to differentiate between the *written version* and the *unwritten reality* of a policy, procedure, or performance standard. The written version describes how things *should* happen; the unwritten version recounts what is *allowed* to happen. Too often, people disbelieve official written words produced within their organizations.

TABLE 1-3 Presentation Standards

	(Part One)	
Presentation Elements:	*LP, P, HP*[a]	*Comments:*
Interesting *introduction* supported by memorable *central idea?*		Introduction:
		Central Idea:
Purpose* differentiated from *client objectives?		Purpose:
		Client Objectives:
Explained the *big picture*? (what is to be covered)		
Logical *content flow* supported by *evidence*? (personal experience, analogy/ metaphor, expert opinion, recent examples, supporting numbers)		
Powerful *conclusion*? (benefits, outcomes, actions)		

TOTAL   Part One
                    +Part Two
                         Average

TABLE 1-3   *(continued)*

Presentation Standards (Part Two)

Personal Habits:	*LP, P, HP*[a]	*Comments:*
Effective eye contact? (e.g., 2 to 3 seconds per person; scan entire room; avoid looking over people's heads; avoid excessive focus on visuals; look at people when answering their questions; avoid prolonged eye contact with demanding or aggressive audience members)		
Effective gestures and use of visual aids? (e.g., vary hand movements; match "sweep" of gestures to importance of concepts; appear natural; avoid fidgeting with clothing, hair, glasses, paper, equipment; stand left and clear of visuals)		Gestures: Visual Aids:
Commanding physical presence? (e.g., stand firmly on both feet; if sitting, sit "centered" in the seat; avoid clinging to equipment; move close to audience, as appropriate)		
Effective voice? (e.g., speed is appropriate; volume is appropriate to physical space and group size; emotion is relevant to topic)		

Part Two

[a]Rating Scale: Low Pass (LP) = improved performance is needed, Pass (P) = competent performance, High Pass (HP) = stellar performance

TABLE 1-4 Sample: Fast Start to Preparing a Presentation	
Five Key Elements	*Sample Presentation Script*
I. Introduction and Central Idea	**Have you been on a team that:** • Disagreed about almost everything? • Finished only when the deadline hit? Teamwork doesn't have to be painful. To avoid pain, *"work the plan!"*
II. Your Purpose versus Client Objectives	My *purpose* is to explain how to avoid *two mistakes* commonly made by teams. *Why should you care?* Your team will present soon. So if you avoid these two mistakes—if you *work the plan*—your team will avoid pain!
III. Big Picture (table of contents)	**Two mistakes occur if a team doesn't:** 1. Reduce issues to a *one-sentence problem statement.* 2. Create a *central idea* before organizing their key points.
IV. Logical Content Flow with Evidence	First, a team without a *problem statement* asks too many questions. Why? Because they don't know exactly what the client wants! A smart team narrows issues down to one simple problem statement. Then Q&A time is well spent. Second, a team without a *central idea* disagrees on solutions. Why? Because they don't know where they're going. A smart team matches strategies and tactics to one central idea. I once saw a team successfully alter a client's desire to remove a family member from his business. The client saw himself as a "hunter" and the family member as a "farmer." The "hunter" captured new business while the "farmer" took care of current clients. This client *wanted* higher profits. How did the team persuade this client? They used a powerful central idea aimed at a problem statement: "every successful business needs explorers and settlers to maximize profit."
V. Conclusion	So, to save time, *work the plan*! Aim at one problem and focus on one central idea. You'll save time and pain!

When this occurs, people operate on two *parallel levels*. Written words (e.g., policies, procedures, memos, and training instructions) are discounted, devalued, or ignored—or even perceived as false. Unwritten words (e.g., rumors, stories from peers and friends) are believed, valued, or gossiped about—and perceived as truth.

TABLE 1-5   Blank: Fast Start to Preparing a Presentation[a]

Five Key Elements	*Presentation Script*
I. Introduction and Central Idea	
II. Your Purpose versus Client Objectives	
III. Big Picture (table of contents)	
IV. Logical Content Flow With Evidence	
V. Conclusion	

[a]A one-minute presentation requires about 15 sentences! Plan your words carefully.

The Manager's Dilemma

Managers have difficulty persuading people to do something "to specification" when everyone knows that another method or standard of quality is allowed. Managers also suffer from people's inherent mistrust of the written organizational word. T. J. Larkin and Sandar Larkin, in their book entitled *Communicating Change: Winning Employee Support for New Business Goals*, cite the work of Philip Marvis and Donald Kanter regarding cynicism in the workplace. They note that ". . . forty-three percent of workers are cynics and . . . these people are not just suspicious, they firmly believe management lies and is trying to cheat them (p. 4)."

An *invisible fourth wall* (i.e., an unseen barrier between communicator and audience) constantly lurks as a veiled shadow in every communication effort. The wall, in effect a barrier to effective communications, lurks in one-to-one communications as well as group scenarios.

A Story Is One Solution

Is there a simple solution to this parallel universe of behaviors and expectations in organizations? There is no single answer; solutions can require iterative evolutions and answers often demand the involvement of the entire organizational structure. However, the fact is that managers always fight against perceptions of expectations versus actual behaviors.

Howard Gardner, Harvard professor and author of *Leading Minds*, was quoted in Thomas Stewart's September 7, 1998, *Fortune* magazine article: Gardner said that stories "constitute the single most powerful weapon in the leader's literary arsenal."

Most people believe in the power of the spoken story, but when it comes to business writing, can a story serve as a powerful and constructive writing tool? The answer is yes and the reasons are straightforward:

- Stories are *memorable*. People recall a story better than they can recount a manager's eight-step plan for improvement. Stories contain action verbs and they have clear beginnings, middles, and ends—all of which make them memorable.
- Stories *tell the truth*. People clarify an organization's real culture and behavioral expectations through anecdotes. Stories prove to people what they can do and what they cannot do within the context of an organization.

Managers might garner more share of mind if they capitalize on two tactics when they write:

- The *art* of telling a *story*.
- The *science* of writing in the *active voice*.

A discussion of writing emphatically in the active voice starts on page 20.
The big picture of how managers write for the greatest impact is twofold:

1. Tell a *story* (the art) to create common ground with readers' *emotions*.
2. Write in the *active voice* (the science) to efficiently cover the *facts*.

Try these tips for telling stories in the active voice and when writing for business in general.

- Use analogies and metaphors so people attach visual images to the message. An *analogy* compares the similar features of two things or concepts; the words *like* or *as* are used in the comparison. A *metaphor* is a figure of speech in which a term or concept is applied to an unrelated thing or concept to illustrate a resemblance.
- Write from the readers' point of view. Readers infer your *tone* from the *style* in which you write (see J. S. Fielden's classic 1982 *Harvard Business Review* article, entitled "What do you mean you don't like my style?"). Readers regard your tone as positive if you write with them in mind; readers perceive your tone as negative if you write with your own purpose in mind.
- Write efficiently to save everyone's time.
- Evaluate your documents against preestablished standards (see the Writing Standards checklist in this chapter).

The Story: Emotions

USE ANALOGIES AND METAPHORS

Readers connect to written documents faster if they can create visual images of the words; excellent teachers of fiction know this to be true when they consistently instruct less experienced writers to "show us, don't tell us."

Try this for an *analogy*. Business writing is like the computer game *Sim City*: When you create a document, you can't imagine all the reactions it will cause! Some people will misinterpret what you meant, others will start rumors, and some will ignore your document entirely. Your job, as manager and author of the document, then becomes damage control. You watch helplessly as a simple written document quickly disintegrates into a complicated communication issue. (For people unfamiliar with this reference, *Sim City* is a computer software game in which you build a city by programming in fire stations, neighborhoods, industrial areas, parks, etc. After you create a city, you can't imagine all the variations of problems and disasters it will cause! Fires start spontaneously, citizens scream about the tax rate, budgets run low. Your job, as mayor and creator of the city, becomes damage control.)

If you've been a manager for any length of time, the written document scenario and aftermath sound all too familiar. The simplest document, written with the most honest of intentions, can cause quite a stir among a percentage of employees. (My theory is that 20 percent of employees usually cause 80 percent of the unnecessary problems; Pareto's Law at work in the world of communications.)

Admittedly, writing is an emotional and difficult process. Your emotions are involved when you write. You want every word to say what you mean. People's emotions are involved when they read what you've written; they may resent being told what to do and they might read things into words that simply weren't intended.

Try this true story from a corporation (with which I'm familiar) as a *metaphor*. A senior management team, literally, climbed a mountain for several days; their purpose was to build a cohesive team and make great changes in their organization when they came home. Mountain climbing may have been a powerful metaphor for team-building and change to *them*, but the employees back home didn't buy it. Some employees didn't see any *truth* in senior management's climbing experience, and employees couldn't visualize a bunch of executives tromping through the wild equating to any operational *value* for their workdays. The resulting change documents fell, all too often, on deaf ears.

If written communication involves so much emotion, then *value* is a critical concept as you try to create a truthful, powerful bridge among people. Many of us think that what motivates us also motivates our employees. Yeah, right.

Sim City (i.e., you don't know what will happen next) is alive and well in written communications. Unless you assume the emotional point of view of the reader and prove value (e.g., benefits) pretty quickly, you'll have a lot to explain later.

Analogies and metaphors help you tell a good story and they cause more people to recall what you want them to remember. As a final benefit, the analogy or metaphor helps sell the truth of your story, much like an effective parable sells the central truth behind a story.

Examples of Analogies and Metaphors

Write from Your Readers' Point of View. People often remember information because the writer connected with them in some way. You can connect with people by establishing a common visual of what you mean and by reaching out to their true emotions. Analogies and metaphors help you paint these illustrations and tap into emotions.

Read these two examples of analogies:

- This year's profits were like a pole vault jumper: They rose sharply but soon fell.
- The structure of your presentation is as solid as the structure of a strong building.

A sample metaphor follows: The audience's reasons for listening and their ability to recall what you said are linked to your planning. You must make it easy to live within the *well-planned walls* of your presentation (referring back to the previous Sarah Winchester house metaphor example in one of this chapter's tables).

Try this two-step exercise (use Table 1-6):

1. List potential topics for written documents (e.g., announce a new product line, communicate a new organizational structure, introduce a new employee recognition and reward program).
2. Brainstorm analogies and metaphors to use when writing about those topics.

When possible, ask other people to brainstorm with you. You'll be surprised by the variety of creative ideas (ideas you'd never think of alone).

If you have difficulty brainstorming such visual comparisons, a nontraditional place to look is *The Oxford-Duden Pictorial English Dictionary*. This book contains terminology, definitions, and illustrations of items, people, equipment, and functions related to almost anything of interest. Categories include animals and plants, community, brewing, atom models, mathematics, musical notation, and household appliances and utensils. This dictionary is one good place to look when you want to start thinking *out of the box* (i.e., creating distance from a personal and somewhat repetitive frame of reference).

Example: Look for Analogies and Metaphors in Speeches

Speeches are great places to find analogies and metaphors. As you watch those sound bites on the daily news, listen carefully to the speakers.

TABLE 1-6 Topics and Potential Analogies or Metaphors

Topics	*Brainstorm List of Analogies and Metaphors*

Consider this scenario: Your organization is downsizing and transferring product managers because of consolidated product lines. Employees are worried; they may lose their jobs. Review the speech-writing examples in Table 1-7. Which *feels* better to you—the poor example or the better example?

Edit a Rough Draft to Include More Visual Images

Review the ideas in Table 1-8 for refining a rough draft into a better speech. The five elements of an effective presentation provide the general structure for the speech. Note how the visual metaphor becomes a strong central idea throughout the speech.

Example: Look for Analogies and Metaphors in Proposals

If you buy the idea of using analogies and metaphors, now conceptualize creative ways to *organize* your written proposals. One creative means of organizing a proposal is to look at how experts in various industries approach their work.

How do researchers approach a project? Generally, they state a hypothesis and then study relevant variables. How do engineers determine why one product is better than another product? They tear down both products to see the inner workings and then identify the differences in product features.

TABLE 1-7   Speech-Writing Examples

Start with a strong central idea.	Poor Example: "Together we can succeed."
Why? Because a central idea must be repeated at least twice during this speech to ensure that people remember the main idea behind *why* the company is restructuring.	(People will lose their jobs! "Together" is a poor choice of words.)
	Better Example: "We'll walk a new path to success." ("Walk" denotes single steps. "Success" gives people hope.)
Use one metaphor throughout the speech.	Poor Example: "We can grow and blossom like a flowering tree."
Why? Because people need to hang on to a picture of a successful future. These hard times scare them. A metaphor helps everyone see a common picture of the future.	(This company will first shrink. The metaphor needs to relate to the issues currently facing everyone.)
A metaphor may be used as your central idea (see above).	Better Example: "Don't throw gasoline on the fire; use water instead."
	(This focuses on today's issues and on *individual* responsibility in minimizing gossip and maximizing working toward success. I witnessed a president successfully use this metaphor.)
Write in a conversational and succinct style.	Poor Example: "It is not as important to realize that we have to make changes, as it is to understand how to make those changes."
Why? Because long sentences come across poorly in a speech. The most effective speeches use short, crisp language—language that places emphasis on certain words.	(Too long to remember!)
	Better Example: "We know *that* we must change. The critical part is *how*." (People can remember this!)

TABLE 1-8   Refining a Rough Draft

Presentation Elements	Tips	Examples
Element 1: Interesting introduction supported by memorable central idea?	The audience won't like this news. Avoid an introduction that might anger people. Your best approach could be company- or industry-based statistics, followed by coaching on how to receive and handle the plan. Then, use a metaphor-based central idea.	**Poor Example:** Thank you for coming to this meeting. I'm sure a coach feels like this when cuts are made from the team. **Better Example:** Thank you for coming to this important meeting. I'll get directly to the point. Our two largest competitors have hit our market share. Our profits dropped 12 percent last quarter. Our profitability and sales volume are on downward trends. So, what can we do? Before I tell you, let me ask you to remember one thing as you hear our plan. (pause) Throw water on the fire, not gasoline. What does that mean? (pause) It means this. Be part of our solution, not part of the problem. Focus on facts.
Element 2: Purpose differentiated from audience objectives?	State your purpose from the audience's point of view (POV). You thereby combine your purpose with their objectives. Three speech purposes: 1. To inform—share knowledge or skill. 2. To persuade—modify opinions or motivate. 3. To entertain—enjoy stories. Repeat a phrasing style: it helps people remember.	**Poor Example:** My purpose is to inform you about changes we are facing. **Better Example:** My purpose today is twofold. First, I want you to be aware of changes caused by the numbers and facts I just mentioned. Second, I want you to become convinced. (pause) Convinced of what? (pause) Convinced that you—yes, all of us—are responsible to help our organization through this difficult time. Convinced that our plan is necessary. So, again. How can you help? (pause) Throw water on the fire, not gasoline. Be part of our solution, not part of the problem. Focus on facts.
Element 3: Explained the big picture?	Remind the audience of the big picture at this point. Summarize numbers and facts from the introduction into one results-based big picture.	**Example:** The numbers and facts are real. If we continue on this path, our competition will win and we will lose profits and market share. That—plain and simple—is the big picture. (pause) We want to paint a new big picture. And we have two strategies to do just that.

(continued)

TABLE 1-8 *(continued)*

Presentation Elements	Tips	Examples
Element 4: Logical content flow supported by evidence? (personal experience, analogy/metaphor, expert opinion, recent examples, supporting numbers)	Explain the steps to be taken in the near future. State when to expect additional information.	**Example:** So. What will we do? First, (here we must note specific steps and dates related to when the changes will occur, to help manage people's perceptions). I will hold another company-wide meeting in two weeks. (pause) The meeting will be on the same day of the week, same time. I'll tell you how our future looks then.
Element 5: Powerful conclusion?	Use *active verbs* that tell people *exactly* what you want them to do during the transition period. Your goal is to motivate people into action. Repeat a phrasing style: It facilitates information recall. Promise many informative meetings: Providing information and repeating it often are necessary in difficult times of organizational transition.	**Poor Example:** I want you to understand our dilemma and help us. **Better Example:** As I conclude, I ask you to do three things: 1. Attend every meeting. If you do, you'll understand the real numbers and facts. 2. Plan your projects carefully. If you do, our clients won't suffer because of our transition. 3. Cooperate like never before. If you do, we will get through this tough time. If you do, we will succeed. In closing, let me repeat how you can help. Throw water on the fire, not gasoline. Be part of our solution, not part of the problem. Focus on facts. Thank you for attending this meeting. Thank you for your cooperation. All managers will hold a meeting tomorrow. You will learn additional details at those meetings. Thank you.

Consider various disciplines as *metaphors* for how to approach a particular proposal. You'll see these ideas in Table 1-9:

1. Traditional proposal—similar to what researchers write as a typical research report.
2. Deconstructionist proposal—similar to what writers and engineers do when they tear a document or a product apart and analyze how to improve it.
3. Reductionist proposal—similar to what physicians do when they analyze symptoms, run tests, diagnose the problem, and recommend a treatment.

**TABLE 1-9 Look for Analogies and Metaphors in Proposals
(Use other disciplines to help you tell *your* proposal story.)**

Use . . .	To tell the story of your proposal in this way:
I. Traditional (research) Purpose: To summarize findings, conclusions, and recommendations.	1. State your introduction and your hypothesis. 2. Note your assumptions (float them to a relevant position in the document). 3. List major findings and the conclusions you've drawn. 4. Outline critical recommendations (i.e., action steps). 5. Conclude by clarifying the benefits to the audience. Illustration and central idea metaphor: stepping stone, experiment, etc.
II. Deconstructionist (literature, engineering) Purpose: To provide a rationale for dismantling the old methodology and implementing the new.	1. State your introduction and provide a background statement (the context). 2. Note your assumptions (float them to a relevant position in the document). 3. Review the current methodology (what works and why, and compliment the creators and implementers of current method). 4. Present ideas for new method (how to and why). 5. Outline a transition plan (who, what, when, where, why, how). 6. Conclude by clarifying the benefits to various stakeholders. Illustration and central idea metaphor: current state versus desired state, etc.
III. Reductionist (medicine) Purpose: To reduce an issue (by reviewing its symptoms) to root cause(s) and to sell a new solution.	1. State your introduction and provide a background statement (the context). 2. Note your assumptions (float them to a relevant position in the document). 3. Use an *if/then statement*: *If* these are the issues and symptoms (analysis), *then* we can make these assumptions about the causes (diagnosis). 4. Outline the necessary strategies and tactics (treatment). 5. Conclude by clarifying the benefits to various stakeholders. Illustration and central idea metaphor: fish bone diagram of causes and effects, etc.
IV. Benchmarking (creative) Purpose: To compare issues in similar or dissimilar organizations and to present a creative solution.	1. State your introduction and note why changes are needed. 2. Note your assumptions (float them to a relevant position in the document). 3. Describe a similar situation in another organization. 4. Note why the two situations are similar and relevant to your need. 5. Outline a transition plan (who, what, when, where, why, how). 6. Conclude by emphasizing the benefits and the expected outcomes. Illustration and central idea metaphor: Venn diagram, paradigm shift from narrow view of products to broader view as provider of industry-leader services, etc.
V. Process Flow (science, engineering) Purpose: To propose a new fact-based process flow.	1. State your introduction and a one-sentence problem statement. 2. Note your assumptions (float them to a relevant position in the document). 3. Visualize the process, noting the locations and causes of any problem points. 4. State how to fix the problem(s). 5. Outline a solution plan (how and when to fix the problem, how to evaluate). 6. Note, as future data are gathered, the increasing benefits of fixing the process. Illustration and central idea metaphor: flow chart, phased-in work plan, etc.

4. Benchmarking proposal—similar to what Southwest Airline's benchmarking team did when they used race car pit crew techniques to help decrease the on-ground turnaround time of their planes.

5. Process flow proposal—similar to what scientists and engineers do when they reengineer a new process flow.

Active Voice: Facts

Write Effectively. The goal of business communications, according to Olivia Stockard (author of *The Write Approach: Techniques for Effective Business Writing*) is to "communicate information clearly to someone who needs that information for the purpose of doing business" (p. 3). That's a simple definition. Because it is simple, it is elegant.

Mary Munter, in her book entitled *Guide to Managerial Communication: Effective Business Writing and Speaking*, notes that ". . . business writers usually write under severe time pressures; therefore, increasing your writing efficiency is extremely important" (p. 35). That's to the point; and that's the way we should write.

People are inundated with numerous communications, through various media, every day. What is the result? Here are the trends that this author sees in written business communications. People often

- delay reading documents that don't seem necessary or urgent (these documents go to the bottom of the in box and too often stay there).
- skim business documents. I know a successful businessperson admitting to reading only the first sentence in every paragraph.
- want to read the bottom line first; they don't have time to wade through all the details.
- neglect formerly required conventions in electronic communications (e.g., correct grammar, capitalization, and spelling).
- misunderstand written communications because voice inflection, facial expressions, and body language are absent.
- feel overwhelmed by the variety and volume of communications (e.g., voice mail, e-mail, Internet, memos, brochures, interoffice notes, quarterly reports, annual reports, financial reports, evaluation reports). Therefore, people read many documents in a cursory fashion.

The trends, especially when compared against previously acceptable business writing styles, clearly illustrate how writing is changing. The recommended letter style in 1949 for the Standard Oil Company of California's *Correspondence Handbook*, for example, was indented paragraphs. Plain type was used; bullet points, boldface, or italics were not seen in letters and memos. Today, depending on the document purpose and the intended audience, letters and memos may contain bold and italic typeface as well as enumerated lists or bullet points. Often, bold headings lead busy readers' eyes through key topical points.

These written business communication trends have not, however, replaced the need for correct grammar, active voice, and the sage advice *say what you mean*. The guidelines in the *Correspondence Handbook* were good in 1949 and are still good today: avoid "due to the fact that" and instead use "because" (p. 75). Why? Because it is simpler.

Write Efficiently. What is efficient writing? Efficient writing, as a concept, means that you start (to borrow a famous phrase from Stephen Covey) with the end in mind.

1. What is your *purpose* for writing? Match your purpose to the document format and writing style.
2. Who will read the document? Match the audience's needs to the document format and writing style.
3. What do you want people to do after reading the document? Again, match intended outcomes to the document format and writing style.

Are you beginning to see a trend? An efficient writer creates a conceptual link between her purpose, the audience's needs, and the intended outcomes before she types 250 words on a page. I find that answering six simple questions can help writers create this conceptual link (see Table 1-10).

An efficient writer answers all these questions, creates a conceptual link in her mind or through a sketch or outline on paper, and then starts writing. Journalism students know this lesson well. Effective writers know that more time devoted to up front planning results in less time wasted in subsequent rewriting and reorganizing.

Let's now look at this six-question process in a different way. Table 1-11 leads you through another way to conceptualize this process.

Being Able to Write Emphatically in the Active Voice. Some MBA students say, "I've never heard of emphatic, active voice. We weren't taught that in school." They are absolutely right. In case you are one of those people, the next paragraph should put emphatic writing and the active voice in perspective.

You see, I forgot to tell you something. You can improve the previous heading, "Being Able to Write Emphatically in the Active Voice" if you use fewer words and start with a more forceful verb. It could read: "Write Emphatically in the Active Voice." Isn't that more memorable and easier to read?

I learned my first active voice writing lesson when employed as an evaluation specialist at Arthur Andersen & Company. I was fresh out of my Ph.D. program and, believe me, most doctoral students don't write dissertations in the active voice. A wonderful manager, Dan, took the time to edit our evaluation reports. I distinctly recall one of the first reports I wrote. I'd received my third set of edits from Dan. I sat in disbelief, but finally my sense of humor took over. I edited the document, paper-clipped a crumpled $10 bill to the front page, and hand delivered the new version to Dan. I said, "If I give you this huge amount of cash, then will you stop editing my report?" (Even then I understood the value of an *if, then* statement!)

TABLE 1-10	Six Simple Questions				
What?	*Who?*	*When?*	*Where?*	*Why?*	*How?*
What is my purpose?	Who will read this (i.e., are there different stakeholders with varying needs)?	When do I want something done (or when did it occur)?	Where are the locations, offices, groups, or people involved?	Why should the readers care?	How do I format the document to maximize the readers' willingness to read?

TABLE 1-11 Another Way to Perceive the Six Simple Questions	
Organize your plan for writing a document as follows:	*Know the answers to these items:*
First, identify your purpose for writing the document.	1. Do you want to inform (e.g., *what*)? 2. Do you need to persuade (e.g., *what*)? 3. Do you want to describe (e.g., *what*)? 4. Do you wish to entertain (e.g., *what*)? Writing for retirement party speeches, achievement celebrations, or "roasts" are examples of business entertainment writing.
Second, given your audience, select the appropriate document design, writing style, and tone.	*Who* are the various stakeholders within your reading audience? Generally (for any purpose): • Use succinct sentences, bullet points, boldface, and italics to emphasize key points so that readers can comprehend the document by skimming it (e.g., *how*). • Clearly emphasize the benefits to the readers (e.g., *why*). If your purpose is to inform: • Describe events chronologically (e.g., *what* and *when*). If your purpose is to persuade: • Include evidence (e.g., statistics, facts, support of experts) to enhance document credibility (e.g., *why*). If your purpose is to describe: • Discuss key points by beginning with the big picture or the historical background and then describing details (e.g., *what*). If your purpose is to entertain: • Create an uncluttered document design (e.g., *how*).
Third, write a draft of the document.	1. Visualize your purpose, the stakeholders of the audience, and the reaction you desire from those stakeholders (e.g., *what, who, when, where, why, how*). 2. Write a quick first draft without agonizing over every word. 3. Spell-check the document. Work on something else for a while. 4. Read the document again and edit as necessary.
Fourth, imagine the readers' reactions.	1. Visualize Pareto's Law (80/20 rule). Imagine that 20 percent of the people read the document thoroughly and 80 percent skim. Edit the document again to ensure that your message is clear and that the document is easy to skim. 2. Imagine that 20 percent of the people cause 80 percent of the negative reactions to the document. Edit the document to eliminate potential tone issues that may cause negative reactions. 3. Ask a trusted colleague to review the document before disseminating.

Dan and I shared a good laugh as he returned the crumpled bill to me. Then Dan took the time to explain the *why* behind his edits: emphatic, active voice writing meant that you avoid (as often as possible) words like *are, make, is, may, do,* and *have.* If you wrote with the fewest (and best) words possible, then you benefited from the simplicity. Emphatic writing and active voice are, simply, more elegant.

Arthur Andersen & Company's motto of "Think Straight, Talk Straight" was not a joke. Dan, manager and patient editor, taught me what it really meant. And Dan, wherever you are, I'm forever grateful. Although, until I grasped the concept of active voice writing, I admit that I personified our underground tag line to the motto: "Work Late, Don't Date!"

Peruse Table 1-12 and see the visible difference between passive voice writing and emphatic, active voice writing. If you grasp the concept, write this way from your first draft. You'll save hours of thinking and editing time. If managers taught employees how to write emphatically in the active voice, everyone would achieve final drafts faster.

Evaluate Documents against Standards

Start with Standards. Editing can be painful. Some of us don't like to write because we don't know how to edit efficiently and effectively. Streamline your editing by evaluating all documents against a common set of criteria. Once you understand where you should aim, in terms of effective writing, the editing process becomes more enjoyable.

A Definition of Evaluation. The purpose of evaluation is to judge *worth*. Worth cannot be measured without first knowing what constitutes worth (e.g., quality, acceptability, and utility). Use Table 1-13 (Writing Standards) as a sample evaluation tool. Writers benefit from seeing edits categorized under specific headings (elements). When writers see trends in their writing, they quickly identify where to spend their greatest efforts in conceptualizing and writing a document.

TABLE 1-12 Passive Voice Versus Emphatic, Active Voice

Passive Voice (A writing style to avoid)	Emphatic, Active Voice (Use this writing style)
• If you use forms of words like *are, make, is, may, do,* and *have* too often, then your sentences sound like *passive voice*. • Words with *-ing* at the end are often indicators of *passive voice*. • Repetitive words, written too close together, sound redundant.	• Fewer words and action-oriented verbs produce *active voice* sentences. • *Active voice* writing varies: 1. Words 2. Sentence structure 3. Sentence openers
Passive Voice Examples	*Emphatic, Active Voice Examples*
This *is* an illustration of the solution.	This illustrates the solution.
He *made* the salesperson give a full accoun*ting* of the time spent on sales calls.	He required the salesperson to fully account for sales call time.
She added more contractors to *make* the construction go faster.	She added more contractors to speed up construction.
Clark *is* in the habit of blaming his staff when something goes wrong.	Clark habitually blames his staff when something goes wrong.
I am thin*king* of making this *recommendation* to the president. *I have* listed my *recommendation* in wri*ting* below. *I* would like to *have* your comments by tomorrow morning.	My proposed recommendation to the president is listed below. Please provide me with your comments by 10:00 A.M. tomorrow morning.
A difficult reconciliation of the different departments *was* attempted by the CEO and chief negotiator.	The CEO and chief negotiator attempted a difficult reconciliation of the various departments.

TABLE 1-13 Writing Standards[a]

Element	*Element*
Effective document design? • Graphic devices: white space, blocks of text, indentations, margins, boldface, underlining, and bulleted or enumerated lists. • Headings: reader-based and in parallel form. • Typography: consistent style, serif font, upper- and lower-case, readable size.	**Well-structured paragraphs?** • Logical: ideas progress in relevant manner. • Topic sentence: states (a) purpose or point of view, (b) concise definition of a problem, (c) lucid statement of key issue or fact. • Key points: one major point per paragraph. • Concise: avoids unnecessary redundancies. • Final paragraph: key conclusion, analysis of problem, concise summary of points, clear opinion, suggestions or solutions, or questions asked of reader.
Coherent, overall? • Opening: creates interest and explains background. • Purpose: communicated early. • Big picture: explained before details are provided. • Closing: ties together all ideas: a key conclusion, final analysis of the problem, concise summary of points, clear statement of opinion or position, specific suggestions or solutions, or specific questions asked of reader.	**Well-structured sentences?** • Structure: concise. • Punctuation: correct. • Spelling: zero defects. • Numbers: written correctly. • Subject and verb agreement: singular; plural; gender-appropriate.
Style and tone appropriate to purpose and context? • Terminology: businesslike. • Voice: active; easy to read. • Jargon: avoided. • Wording: tactful; targeted to audience(s) and purpose.	**In a sentence, what is your *reaction* to the document?**

[a]Continuum of evaluation ratings:
- Low Pass (LP) = improved performance needed
- Pass (P) = competent performance
- High Pass (HP) = stellar performance

The Writing Standards are divided into five elements:

1. Document design
2. Overall coherence
3. Style and tone (as measured against purpose and context)
4. Paragraph structure
5. Sentence structure

Now, practice using the Writing Standards by completing this exercise:

1. Review the Writing Standards.
2. Evaluate the Sample Letter (to edit!) on the subsequent page.
3. Then review the Evaluation of the sample letter.

Read the Sample Letter. Errors reflect the mistakes found in the source document. First, evaluate this document against the five elements in the Writing Standards. Second, discuss suggested edits and why you recommend them. (See the table entitled "Evaluation" for an outline of this evaluation process and outcomes.)

BOX 1-1

Sample Letter

Dear XXX:

Thank you for being our customer recently. We have grown because of clients like you. We are dedicated to serve you. We have attended three national conferences and have decided to incorporate much of what we learned there into the projects that we deliver to you.

Our people have increased their skills and our cost structures have expanded. Therefore, we must increase our rates by a fraction. Hourly rates for Project Managers have increased from $30.00 per hour to $35.00 per hour. Hourly rates for Senior Project Managers will increase from $50.00 to $55.00 per hour. This change is mandatory for our future success and we feel the increased value of our services will compliment this small change.

Again, we truly appreciate your business and we will continue to improve what we provide to you in the way of services and deliverables. Please do not hesitate to call Sam at 000-0000 if you would like to discuss this further.

Sincerely,

XXX

TABLE 1-14 Evaluation

Review the table below for an outline of the evaluation comments.

Writing Standards: *Element*	*Grade*[a]	*Analyze the Facts and Emotions (F&Es) and Design the Strategy*
Document Design	LP	Yes, this is a letter. Don't you write letters in paragraphs? Not always. If the company announces a rate increase in a letter, strong benefits must appear early (i.e., what's in it for customers). Highlight what's important to customers through headings, bold typeface, and italicized words. Otherwise, customers' eyes are drawn first to the numbers.
Overall Coherence	LP	The letter is not coherent. Readers compare the rate increase against a vague claim of service enhancements. Readers feel like generic clients: The purpose is unclear, there is no big picture, and the closing is weak. Customers have no "you are here" marker anywhere in the letter—except to know that they'll write bigger checks now!
Style and Tone	LP	Active voice is not alive and well in this document. Note the number of times *have, are,* and *will* clutter sentences. This letter targets customers, but the tone does not. The letter is written from the point of view of the company. Do customers care about the number of conferences attended? No, customers care about the impact on their needs.
Paragraph Structure	LP	Ideas don't progress in a logical manner; topic sentences don't foreshadow the meaning of paragraphs. There is clearly only one key point: rates increased!
Sentence Structure	LP	Sentences suffer from wordiness and passive voice.
Your Reaction	—	I, as a client, mistrust the credibility of this organization and resent the vague attempt to rationalize a rate increase. (Result? The company just shot itself in the foot.)

[a]Continuum of evaluation ratings:
  • Low Pass (LP) = improved performance needed
  • Pass (P) = competent performance
  • High Pass (HP)= stellar performance

CASES

CASES

Before you work the cases found on the following pages, please review the section of this casebook entitled "How to Use This Book and Work the Cases." There is no single best solution; the organizational context, politics, and personalities involved always affect what comprises the best solution for the situation. The true value of the cases rests with your ability to:

1. Conceptualize new methods of problem solving.
2. Consider many alternatives, from others' points of view.
3. Analyze the assumptions you make about the cases—and why you didn't make certain assumptions.
4. Participate in discussions about the cases, if possible, to see how others would solve the issues.

Case 1-1   Organizational Structure Memo

(Case purpose: Evaluate an organizational change memo and its impact on staff.)

STEP 1: REVIEW THE BIG PICTURE

Assume that the text in Box 1-2 is your first rough draft of a memo to employees in your department. First, evaluate this document against the five elements in Table 1-15. Second, discuss suggested edits and why you recommend them.

STEP 2: ANALYZE THE FACTS & EMOTIONS (F&Es) AND STEP 3: DESIGN THE STRATEGY

Table 1-16 contains a sample evaluation of the memo. Recall from reading "How to Use This Book and Work the Cases" that F&E is the acronym for Facts and Emotions—because every case requires an analysis of the facts as well as people's emotions.

BOX 1-2

Rough Draft

TO: Staff
FROM: Department VP
RE: Group Structure

Changes have taken place recently that impact the manner in which we will organize staff in the near future. This letter is to explain to you about how we envision structuring our group in the coming FY.

Change can be challenging; we have an opportunity to examine how we have been doing things and how we may make further changes to alter our organization and impact results. Our mission needs to be kept foremost in our minds whenever we look at our structure. The first step taken towards change to achieve more efficiency and strength began recently.

We just have not seen enough revenue growth over the past two years. And, when we look at all the costs, our expenses are just too high. For these reasons, we will decrease our department staffing by three people in the next month. All three people will be transferred into comparable positions in other divisions of the company.

Why is this necessary? Our vision is to be the best. We must change. We want to continue business profitably for the next 25 years. So, if you need to contact us in the future, call me. Please call with any questions; we know that change creates new issues but we are here to work together.

TABLE 1-15   Case 1-1: Writing Standards Checklist

Element:	*LP, P, HP*[a]	*Element:*	*LP, P, HP*[a]

Effective document design?
- Graphic devices: white space, blocks of text, indentations, margins, boldface, underlining, and bulleted or enumerated lists.
- Headings: reader-based and in parallel form.
- Typography: consistent style, serif font, upper- and lower-case, readable size.

Well-structured paragraphs?
- Logical: ideas progress in relevant manner.
- Topic sentence: states a) purpose or point of view, b) concise definition of a problem, or c) lucid statement of key issue or fact.
- Key points: one major point per paragraph.
- Concise: avoids unnecessary redundancies.
- Final paragraph: key conclusion, analysis of problem, concise summary of points, clear opinion, suggestions or solutions, or questions asked of reader.

Coherent, overall?
- Opening: creates interest and explains background.
- Purpose: communicated early.
- "Big picture": explained before details are provided.
- Closing: ties together all ideas; e.g., a key conclusion, final analysis of the problem, concise summary of points, clear statement of opinion or position, specific suggestions or solutions, or specific questions asked of reader.

Well-structured sentences?
- Structure: concise.
- Punctuation: correct.
- Spelling: zero defects.
- Numbers: written correctly.
- Subject and verb agreement: singular; plural; gender-appropriate.

Style and tone appropriate to purpose and context?
- Terminology: businesslike.
- Voice: active; easy to read.
- Jargon: avoided.
- Wording: tactful; targeted to audience(s) and purpose.

In a sentence, what is your *reaction* to the document?

---

[a]Continuum of evaluation ratings:
- Low Pass (LP) = improved performance needed
- Pass (P) = competent performance
- High Pass (HP) = stellar performance

TABLE 1-16 Sample Evaluation

Writing Standards: Element	Grade[a]	Analyze the F&Es and Design the Strategy
Document Design	P	The format fits a typical (if somewhat outdated) internal memo: paragraphs and no formatting beyond the *to, from,* and *subject.* In this case, fancy design work would detract from the message—and probably insult the readers. (The VP should hold a meeting instead.)
Overall Coherence	P	The letter is somewhat coherent. The VP moves from describing change, to outlining poor organizational results, to how these variables necessitate moving people out of the department. However, readers are still uneasy about what's really between the lines.
Style and Tone	LP	Active voice is not alive and well in this document. Note the number of times *have, are,* and *will* clutter sentences. A department (comprised of people with feelings!) resents the tone of the letter because the style is wrong. The VP sounds cold and uncaring.
Paragraph Structure	P	Ideas progress somewhat logically, yet only one key point remains—three people are going on a long trip!
Sentence Structure	LP	Sentences suffer from wordiness and passive voice.
Your Reaction	—	I, as an employee, could mistrust the credibility of my VP because the VP didn't speak to us face-to-face; I have more questions than answers at this point.
		(Result? The VP just wrote a letter that does more damage than good; employees want a meeting and answers. And, now they're angry about one more thing—the letter!)

[a]Continuum of evaluation ratings:
- Low Pass (LP) = improved performance needed
- Pass (P) = competent performance
- High Pass (HP) = stellar performance

* Case 1-2   Evaluation Report

(Case purpose: Evaluate a direct report's ability to communicate succinctly in writing.)

STEP #1: REVIEW THE BIG PICTURE

You are a busy senior manager in this case. You delegate the task of revising your division's standard operating procedures (SOP) manual to a subordinate. The subordinate asks you to approve the sample evaluation report format (in Table 1-17) before she evaluates the entire manual and writes her recommendations. Your task is to decide whether this format tells you what to change in the manual (use Table 1-18). Your response to the subordinate could be any of the following (select one):

1. Yes, this format works well. Proceed and write your report to me in this manner.
2. This format works pretty well. Make these changes to the format and then proceed with the evaluation of our manual.
3. No, this format doesn't work for me. This is what I'd like the report to look like.

STEP 2: ANALYZE THE FACTS & EMOTIONS (F&Es) AND STEP 3: DESIGN THE SOLUTION

TABLE 1-17   Evaluation Format

Document	Findings and Conclusions: By Section/Content	Recommendations
Department XYZ's Standard Operating Procedures Manual	**Quality Control Checklist** • The Quality Control Checklist clearly delineates specific indicators of quality and respective quality acceptance levels. • No sample scenarios are provided.	1. Continue using the Quality Control Checklist (see Appendix for updates). 2. Document sample scenarios to include in the Procedures section. 3. Train new employees (via on-the-job training) using the Quality Control Checklist and sample scenarios. 4. Train new employees on the line, asking them to refer to the Quality Control Checklist and Sample Scenarios. 5. Build Sample Scenarios by observing new employees during training and interviewing experienced employees.

TABLE 1-18 Case 1-2: Writing Standards Checklist		

Element:	*LP, P, HP[a]*	*Element:*	*LP, P, HP[a]*
Effective document design?		**Well-structured paragraphs?**	
• Graphic devices: white space, blocks of text, indentations, margins, boldface, underlining, and bulleted or enumerated lists.		• Logical: ideas progress in relevant manner.	
• Headings: reader-based and in parallel form.		• Topic sentence: states a) purpose or point of view, b) concise definition of a problem, or c) lucid statement of key issue or fact.	
• Typography: consistent style, serif font, upper- and lower-case, readable size.		• Key points: one major point per paragraph.	
		• Concise: avoids unnecessary redundancies.	
		• Final paragraph: key conclusion, analysis of problem, concise summary of points, clear opinion, suggestions or solutions, or questions asked of reader.	
Coherent, overall?		**Well-structured sentences?**	
• Opening: creates interest and explains background.		• Structure: concise.	
• *Purpose:* communicated early.		• Punctuation: correct.	
• "Big picture": explained before details are provided.		• Spelling: zero defects.	
• *Closing:* ties together all ideas; e.g., a key conclusion, final analysis of the problem, concise summary of points, clear statement of opinion or position, specific suggestions or solutions, or specific questions asked of reader.		• Numbers: written correctly.	
		• Subject and verb agreement: singular; plural; gender-appropriate.	
Style and tone appropriate to purpose and context?		**In a sentence, what is your *reaction* to the document?**	
• Terminology: businesslike.			
• Voice: active; easy to read.			
• Jargon: avoided.			
• Wording: tactful; targeted to audience(s) and purpose.			

[a]Continuum of evaluation ratings:
• Low Pass (LP) = improved performance needed
• Pass (P) = competent performance
• High Pass (HP) = stellar performance

TABLE 1-19 Solution

Writing Standards: Element	Grade[a]	Analyze the F&Es and Design the Strategy
Document Design	HP	I'm a busy senior manager! I love this format because it is easy to skim and I know exactly what to do to improve our standard operating procedures manual.
Overall Coherence	HP	I could revise our manual simply by handing the current manual and the evaluation report to a trusted employee and delegating the entire task.
Style and Tone	HP	Active voice dominates this document: every recommendation starts with a verb. I don't need special catering to my emotions in this report; I'm more interested in the facts of how to improve the manual. (Even if I drafted the current manual, the succinct format of this document is unlikely to offend me—unless I'm pathetically insecure.)
Paragraph Structure	HP	Ideas progress somewhat logically in a succinct manner.
Sentence Structure	P	A conversational style is not part of the report; however, that style would only clutter my bottom line needs.
Your Reaction	—	I, as the senior manager, accept the report format as effective and efficient.
		(Result? The senior manager implements most of the recommended enhancements because they *appear* easy to implement in the evaluation report; this is a function of the design.)

[a]Continuum of evaluation ratings:
- Low Pass (LP) = improved performance needed
- Pass (P) = competent performance
- High Pass (HP) = stellar performance

Case 1-3   Stop (i.e., Edit) J!

(Case purpose: Coach a direct report toward better writing.)

STEP 1: REVIEW THE BIG PICTURE

Assume that you are a manager in a corporation. One of your direct reports drafted the memo in Box 1-3; we'll call your employee "J." The memo is intended for distribution under the corporate president's signature, Pat Clark.

BOX 1-3

Memo Draft 1

To: Corporate Employees and Managers
From: Pat Clark, President
Date: (Today's date)
Subject: Needed Training

At our annual meeting last week, I told all of you that we would work to continuously improve our customer service. At this time, I'd like to review our plans and explain why this is an extremely important undertaking for our corporation.

We want you to become "experts" in your professional disciplines. Starting this month, we are placing the first course on our corporate Intranet system. This course is part of a system by which all people will be trained and tested in the knowledge and skills required for our jobs.

When you complete the training, it tells you, our customers, and me that you are an expert in our products and services. You will be asked to read a self-study and take a test (via your computer). You must finish the self-study and test. The class zeroes in on applying our products and services to client problems. So, find the self-study on the Intranet and take the test. Happy studying and good luck!

First, revise the memo: edit the style, tone, format, and grammar. This memo could benefit from massive editing! Can you rewrite it to get employees to be curious about the benefits of participating in training? Can you use an *analogy* or *metaphor* to illustrate why the training benefits both employees and customers?

Second, write a note to "J" stating what you edited and why. Can you write the note to preserve J's ego—so J doesn't get angry or feel defeated before you have a chance to speak with J in person?

STEP 2: ANALYZE FACTS AND EMOTIONS (F&Es)

First, the Facts. J clearly doesn't understand the key features of writing for a corporate audience, such as how to:

- Write persuasively.
- Format a document for busy people.
- Make a leader sound credible.

Second, the Emotions. J misjudged the corporate reading audience. How many managers and employees jump at the chance to spend their copious free time completing required training? People often view corporate training as a nuisance and as an activity that interferes with their real work. This memo, though well-intentioned, simply fuels their resentment. In fact, this memo probably leads to actual resistance, procrastination, and refusal to complete the required training.

If you were J's seasoned manager, what would you do? You'd probably coach J on the facts and emotions of drafting such a memo for the president's signature. And, if you valued your job, you'd only send a significantly revised version to the president for his or her review. You'd assume the points of view of the president *and* the employees and you'd think about what arouses interest from both points of view.

For example, is the president a long distance runner? Does the president advocate teamwork and customer satisfaction? If yes, then capitalize on those personal preferences. What motivates your employee population? Are they accustomed to an incentive plan that ties customer satisfaction ratings to their bonus structure? If yes, then sell the required training by telling them what's in it for them.

STEP 3: DESIGN THE STRATEGY

J drafted a second memo. How does this memo (see Box 1-4), written from a charismatic president's point of view, feel to you? Your emotional reaction to the memo tells

---

BOX 1-4

Memo Draft 2

To: Corporate Employees and Managers
From: Pat Clark, President
Date: (Today's date)
Subject: Improved Services for Customers, Benefits for You!

What do I think about when I run? Problems, plans, and solutions. At our annual meeting last week, we talked about how, as a united team, we could improve our customer service. I listened to your ideas and blended them into our new training plans. What was the result? A plan that is a unique solution to (a) our declining customer satisfaction scores, and (b) your desire to enjoy meaningful work! Let me explain.

Our enhanced product and service lines help us deliver satisfaction to our customers. The fastest way to learn new product and service information is through our corporate Intranet. On Monday, when you open your e-mail, you'll receive an invitation to complete the first course in your new training program. The process is simple:

Go online to enroll.
Complete the online self-study.
Complete the quick online test.

What are the benefits to you? You'll receive special recognition from me if you complete the course and test by the end of this month. And, if our customer satisfaction scores rise by two points (on our ten-point scale) by the end of this fiscal year, we'll enjoy a special corporate party. Our customers will be happy. You will be happy. And, when I'm running, I can work on new problems, plans, and solutions. Thank you team. I'm going online on Monday afternoon.

---

much about whether or not the style and resulting tone are on target. There are many edits that could be made: Discuss ways to improve the letter.

Your second task was to write a note to "J." Draft a note to J that preserves J's ego by:

- Beginning with a thank you to J for the effort
- Using a soft and conversational tone
- Explaining why training might result in success (e.g., "if our employees value the program")
- Accepting some of the ownership of the problems in the first draft
- Assuring J that great writing is within the realm of possibilities

It is the author's experience that a few students occasionally express negative opinions about "accepting some of the responsibility" for this writing fiasco; they feel that J's lack of writing skills are J's problem. This may be true, in the abstract, but it is not true in the real life of corporate culture. A manager has, basically, three alternatives when faced with an employee lacking in skills:

1. Ignore J's performance problem (and continue to deal with the symptoms of the root cause).
2. Do the work for J and don't explain why there is a problem (and continue to deal with the symptoms of the root cause).
3. Supply an improved version and coach J on what is different and why it is better (and hope that J has the competencies to learn). Also, consider sending J to a writing clinic.

The only viable alternative is number three and, yes, it takes the most amount of a manager's time (in the short term). Over the long term, however (assuming J was the right hire for the right job), the manager's time would be reduced because the root cause is identified (i.e., writing deficiencies).

The smart manager has a strong enough ego to:

1. Take the time to develop J's skills. After all, isn't one function of a manager to develop the skills of employees?
2. Approach the problem from two points of view: the manager's and the employee's—with one goal in mind—effective and efficient writing!

Smart Managers Develop Their Employees' Skills. If the manager in this case assumed that J is not smart enough to write better, then that manager would never have tried to coach J. This could be a serious error in judgment (i.e., perception) for the manager, especially if J is a valued employee when considering other performance criteria.

John S. Fielden wrote a classic *Harvard Business Review* article in 1982 entitled "What Do You Mean You Don't Like My Style?" Fielden notes that "When they (managers) do route writing assignments to assistants, superiors could save much valuable time and prevent mutual distress if they told the subordinates what style seemed strategically wise in each situation. Playing guessing games also wastes money" (p. 9).

Smart Managers Consider Two Points of View and State One Goal. Many of us try to solve problems by repeating the same arguments. We think that if we can just convince the other person (e.g., force him or her to listen to our logic), then we'll achieve our desired goal.

Jay Conger, in a 1998 *Harvard Business Review* article, says that there are four ways managers fail to persuade:

1. Using a "hard sell."
2. Resisting "compromise."
3. Thinking "the secret of persuasion lies in presenting great arguments."
4. Assuming "persuasion is a one-shot effort."

The smart manager wants J to write better and more efficiently (the goal). A savvy manager sees that J truly doesn't know how to write better (at this point). The smart manager coaches, sends J to a writing class, and perhaps assigns a mentor to J. Then, if these steps don't achieve the goal, the manager looks to other reasons for the performance gap.

Case 1-4   The Conceptual Sell
(Case purpose: Write to capture busy executives' attention.)

STEP 1: REVIEW THE BIG PICTURE

The report in this case (Box 1-5) was authored by a team of middle managers tasked with benchmarking processes for their division. The benchmarking team wants their senior managers to consider ideas and discuss those ideas in detail at an upcoming meeting.

Can you rewrite this *conceptual sell* document to get senior management curious about the benefits of the new ideas? Use an analogy or metaphor to illustrate why the new concept benefits your employees and customers.

STEP 2: ANALYZE FACTS AND EMOTIONS (F&Es)

First, the Facts. This benchmarking team doesn't even get to first base! Their reading audience for this preliminary report is *senior* management! How many senior managers do much beyond skim the written word? They are just too busy to read wordy documents.

Second, the Emotions. Because senior managers are so busy, they want the answer first and the benefits second. Last, they want to understand how all this will happen.

Basically, the document needs a new format and a new sequence of ideas. Try reading the revised version of the report. Would the benchmarking team have a better chance, with this version, of persuading senior management to expend the resources necessary to implement a new system?

STEP 3: DESIGN THE STRATEGY

The new report draft (Box 1-6) is somewhat more persuasive but *far* from final. Discuss your ideas for further edits to the draft document below.

BOX 1-5

Conceptual Sell

Our benchmarking team was formed after our customer satisfaction ratings dropped continually over the past 4 quarters. Our team identified the causes and we now want to use the best practice information we've learned to turn the trend line upwards again.

The root cause of our declining customer satisfaction is our order inquiry system. The current system is a paper-based system in which many "hand-offs" occur. This results in slow process time lines and increased chances for human error.

Our team recommends that we switch the order inquiry system to a computerized database system. The advantages are as follows. First, simple orders could be fulfilled immediately. Product specifications would be stored and automatically "matched" through the database. The benefits would be enhanced customer satisfaction and, eventually, increased sales. Second, complex orders could be easily tracked through the database. We could track trends and purchasing habits and soon contact clients on a proactive basis.

The new system would pay for itself in 6 months. Details will follow at our next meeting. Immediate expenses include system installation and maintenance, and employee training. We ask that you consider our ideas; we'll discuss feasibility at our next session.

BOX 1-6

All Systems Go!

BACKGROUND

We recommend that we phase out our current order inquiry system and phase in a new computerized system. Why? Our benchmarking team formed after our customer satisfaction declined (a trend that continued for four quarters). Our team identified the cause and we want to use the best practice information we've learned to reverse the customer satisfaction trend.

ISSUES AND OUTCOMES

The root cause of our declining customer satisfaction is our current paper-based order inquiry system. Why do we say that our order inquiry system is the root cause of our clients' dissatisfaction? The negative outcomes of our paper-based system tell the story:

- Many hand-offs of paper.
- Slow process time lines.
- Increased chance for human error.
- Lower customer satisfaction.

WE RECOMMEND: ALL SYSTEMS GO!

All Systems Go, as a concept, encompasses two strategies:

Box 1-6 (*continued*)

1. Discontinue the current, paper-based system.

2. Implement a new computerized database system.

WHAT ARE THE BENEFITS?

If we streamline our order inquiry system through a computerized database, we will:

1. Respond immediately to simple product inquiries.

2. Store and match all product specifications automatically through the database.

3. Enhance customer satisfaction.

4. Track and route complex product inquiries through the database.

5. Eliminate the labor-intensive nature of the paper-based system.

6. Track trends and purchasing habits and eventually increase sales.

WE WILL DETERMINE FEASIBILITY NEXT

The new system would pay for itself in just 6 months. Immediate expenses include system installation, system maintenance, and employee training. We ask that you consider our ideas; we will discuss feasibility details at our next session. Soon, we hope to have *All Systems Go!*

Case 1-5   Reading Between Candidates' Lines

(Case purpose: Analyze what job applicants are really trying to say—or hide.)

STEP 1: REVIEW THE BIG PICTURE

Assume that you've opened a middle level secretarial position; two people sent the letters in Boxes 1-7 and 1-8. The position requires strong writing skills (you depend on this person to write first drafts of letters to customers and other field offices), excellent interpersonal skills, strong budgeting skills, and an ability to balance numerous concurrent tasks. Read the body of the letters and respond to the three items below. Your purpose is to screen these candidates; you only want to spend precious time interviewing strong candidates.

Let your curiosity drive your analysis of each candidate. For example, look behind the writing and imagine the person. What would it be like to work with each candidate on a daily basis? How might each candidate respond to a typical work crisis in which your secretary's professionalism makes the difference between a positive or a negative perception of you and your department?

BOX 1-7

Letter 1: Written by a secretary working in another department within your organization.

(Note: This candidate's current manager highly recommended this person when you called to verify the reference.)

(Heading, date, and salutation are missing for the purposes of this exercise.)

— — — — — — — — — — — — — — — —

I would like to apply for the secretarial position you have open. I am currently working for V. Buckley, Vice President of Operations, in our Chesterfield office. I have worked for V. Buckley since joining our firm eighteen months ago. I have found my experience to be very enjoyable.

I've worked in the clerical field for a total of 10 years. I now want more of a challenge. My strong points are that I am good with people, I am very gregarious. I also like doing different types of work every day, so that I don't get bored. In the past, I worked for a local newspaper, where I took pictures for human-interest stories and wrote captions. I now manage our office budget and am responsible for supervising two clerical.

I'd like to come in for an interview as soon as possible. I can drive to your office if I know ahead of time (it takes me about 30 minutes to make the drive). I look forward to meeting you; I have heard that it is fun to work in your department. My work number is extension #5-0000.

Sincerely,

B. E.

---

1. List the strengths and weaknesses of Letter 1 and Letter 2.
2. Note any political issue that could be a factor.
3. List the value judgments you've already made about each applicant's future performance.

STEP 2: ANALYZE FACTS AND EMOTIONS (F&Es)

An efficient way to analyze candidates is to create a *matrix of key variables* and *a shorthand system for rating each person*. The smart manager asks others in the department to review candidates' application materials. A screening team comprised of two or three people can often detect what really lies behind the written words!

STEP 3: DESIGN THE STRATEGY

Candidate 1—B. E.: Candidate 1 (B. E.) is not your best candidate, in spite of the glowing recommendation from B. E.'s current manager. This is a case where you don't want

BOX 1-8

Letter 2: Written by a secretary working in another company.

(Note: You will call to verify references after you interview this person.)

The purpose of my letter is to introduce myself and request an interview for your secretarial job opening ("Secretary: Level B"). I have worked in the secretarial field for 8 years; all of that time has been at Defoe Consulting. I first worked as a Support Secretary for the Senior Consulting Team in Clayton; I now work for L. Dietz, VP of the Clayton Consulting Office.

Defoe Consulting is moving their branch office to Chesterfield. I would prefer to work in a central location since I live near Forest Park and Washington University. I was trained at Meramec Community College; I earned an Associate's degree in Office Supervision. My current job requires that I supervise two clerical people, edit all senior management correspondence, and manage the office budget, among other duties.

I would appreciate the opportunity to interview for this job. You may reach me at 821-0000 during the day or 835-0000 in the evening. Thank you.

Sincerely,

J. A.

TABLE 1-20   Matrix of Key Variables

Variables	Letter 1 Candidate B. E.	Letter 2 Candidate J. A.
Strengths?	• Gregarious • Manager recommendation • Long clerical tenure • Supervisory experience • Likes multiple tasks • Lists current manager	• Letter is structured well • Concise and professional writing • Relevant education • Specific reasons for desire in job • Supervisory experience
Weaknesses?	• Too gregarious? • Differentiating skills? • Casual writing style • Does not quantify any results or success stories	• Does not offer to call us • Does not quantify any results or success stories
Political issues?	• Why is current manager really recommending this person? • Do we have to hire an internal candidate?	(Not sure there are any.)
Curiosity leads me to wonder if this candidate would . . .	• Get bored easily? • Play more than work?	• Be a professional asset to department? • Desire salary in keeping with our rate?
My bottom line opinion is that we should . . .	Do not interview unless test results are superior.	Interview upon test results.

to go on the *facts* of the recommendation; instead, you want to delve into the *emotional* reasons behind such a recommendation. Mr. or Ms. Current Manager probably wants to unload this clerical person. B. E. can be quite gregarious and fun, but work probably comes second to having that fun!

Why do most people react this way to B. E.? B. E.'s letter writing skills do not provide the necessary evidence that B. E. is an excellent secretary.

So what if the internal powers in your organization pressure you to interview B. E.? Well, you'd wisely insist that all candidates complete a battery of assessment tests (after submitting application papers and before qualifying for interviews). The tests, comprised of writing samples, typing tests, production of PowerPoint presentation slides, and other tasks relevant to the job, often weed this kind of candidate out for you. Hence, your political battle is over before it started.

Candidate 2—J. A.: This candidate is the better candidate for an interview, even though this person is an unknown to you. Of course, you'd want this candidate to complete the assessment tests to ensure that he or she does, in fact, possess the skills your job opening requires. But, on the face of it, this candidate has much stronger writing skills and a more professional approach.

Case 1-6   What Did That Consultant Say?

(Case purpose: Consider a consultant's fit with your organization.)

STEP 1: REVIEW THE BIG PICTURE

In this case, you are an executive with a small company. You need to enhance market research and customer satisfaction research strategies. You wish to contract with a consultant who will complement your personality and strengths. The consultant must understand research design, methodology, and analysis; you'd like a consultant who can coach you through your corporate strategic planning process.

You just received a cold-call letter from a consultant (Box 1-9). Your first thought is, "Just in time!" However, take the time to read the body of the letter, discuss potential pros and cons in a small (executive) team, and then decide whether or not you want to call this consultant in for an interview.

As a small team (three to five students or colleagues): Discuss your (executive) team's personalities and working style preferences. Discuss whether this consultant is worth interviewing, and why (or why not).

Cold-Call Letter
(Heading, date, and salutation are missing for the purposes of this exercise.)

The purpose of this letter is to introduce myself and to discuss the potential fit between your organization and my consulting company. My market research consulting practice works with major firms with similar interests and objectives. My MBA and practical experience (15 years as a manager, senior executive, and consultant) will add value to your organization's results.

For the past 7 years, I have owned and operated Smith Consulting & Associates; our specialty is the design and implementation of customized qualitative and quantitative research methodologies. Our client base ranges throughout the United States, Canada, and Asia. A sampling of our projects finds us focusing on consumer brand positioning, product pricing, and brand loyalty.

Prior to forming my consulting practice, I served as Vice President/General Manager of the Synthe-R One Division of Synthe-R Co., the leading manufacturer of synthetic rubber used in automobile tire inner tubes. I led the reorganization of that division, reducing expenses and increasing overall profits for the division.

I enjoy owning a consulting practice because it allows me to creatively apply my analytical skills to a variety of issues and questions. My goal is to utilize my operational knowledge and experience to develop short- and long-term solutions with a few select clients.

I would appreciate the opportunity to meet with you at your convenience and discuss how we might review your organization's goals and results. I have several completed projects, with data portraying solid results, available for review and discussion. I will call you within the next two weeks; thank you.

Sincerely,

Don Smith

As an individual:

1. Write your own one-page cold-call letter. Use information from your curriculum vitae.
2. Circulate your letter among your team members; ask each member to write editorial ideas on your letter.

STEP 2: ANALYZE THE FACTS AND EMOTIONS (F&Es) AND STEP 3: DESIGN THE STRATEGY

Can you analyze a consultant's expertise through a letter? To some extent you can. If you apply the traditional journalism questions of *who, what, when, where, why,* and *how,* you may identify critical information hidden behind Don's words. You may also identify probing questions to ask when speaking with the candidate.

We aren't picking on consultants in this case. The issue *is specificity in written language*. You take on a most difficult task when you draft a letter. Every single sentence must *support* your purpose, *add value* to the overall meaning, and *clarify* your intended outcomes of the letter.

When critiquing Don's letter we can sit back, safely, and play armchair quarterback against his game plan. The benefit in evaluating Don's letter is that we learn something about our writing before *our* credibility is on the line.

TABLE 1-21	The Information Behind the Words
Question	**The Letter Tells Me That . . .**
Who?	✓ Don is a one-person show and he may like it that way. Look at the number of times the words "I" and "my" are mentioned: at least a dozen, and the number of times that professional collaboration is mentioned: none! Your key question should be: "Do I (my executive team) want to collaborate with a loner?" ✓ Note how Don uses "our." "Our specialty," "our client base," and "our organization" are throwaway phrases designed to make readers think there are employees. Nowhere else in the document does Don mention any team members!
What?	✓ What, specifically, has Don accomplished? He provides no specific results or outcome statements. "Reducing expenses" and "increasing overall profits" is fine: but by *how much* and in *what time frame*?
When?	✓ Don's approach to his work history is chronologically confused: he shifts from his consulting practice, to his previous experience, back to his consulting practice. You should ask yourself if his approach to consulting is as confused!
Where?	✓ Yes, Don's clients cover three countries. However, you don't have critical answers such as which industries and companies. Is there a root cause (e.g., lack of credible skills) behind Don's vague approach?
Why?	✓ Why did Don select your company? Perhaps the answer is that he sends letters out to every company! That should worry you; your small company has limited resources and thus needs a true expert.
How?	✓ *How* does Don apply his "analytical skills to a variety of issues and questions" through his "operational knowledge" and skills? The bottom line for this letter is this: Don is a vague guy and you need specific consulting answers. He is probably not a good fit for your organization. Your motto: Client beware! At the least, ask Don for additional documentation and references.

Case 1-7 Rejection Letter Dilemma

(Case purpose: Diplomatically inform a peer of a problem in his/her department.)

STEP 1: REVIEW THE BIG PICTURE

Assume that you're concerned about the quality of recruits interviewing with your organization (you're a senior manager over the operations division). A friend's daughter recently interviewed with your organization. Her report now has you worried about a problem of a different nature (yet related to your original concerns). She said:

1. "The interview was not organized; questions were elementary and didn't require applicants to demonstrate problem solving and idea generation skills."
2. "I met with the manager of the group for which I was qualified; however, I did not have an opportunity to meet with potential coworkers."
3. "The HR representative was rude and had limited interpersonal skills."
4. "I received an *unsigned photocopy* of a rejection letter! It was poorly written with typographical errors. The handwritten envelope address did not match the address on the letter."

Your friend's daughter, in reality, has exceptional skills. She's accepted another position with a respected international organization. Your task is to:

- Review the rejection letter in question (see Box 1-10). Draft what you'd communicate (i.e., probably via a conversation) to the director of human resources. Your purpose is to address the sloppy recruiting practices before your organization's reputation is seriously tarnished. Your tone must reflect your intent to start a solution, not a war!
- Discuss strengths and weaknesses of your team members' ideas for approaching this dilemma.

Note to readers: Perhaps you can't believe this happened, but one of my stellar MBA students did experience this and the company is a well-established international organization.

People working with this case must first discuss assumptions about:

- The relative power between the director of human resources and the manager troubleshooting the issue.
- The risks involved in opening the discussion.
- Methods for persuading the director of human resources (e.g., I'm not escalating this issue, instead I came to you first; our company's reputation is at stake; I've been impressed with the improvements you've made to the HR function thus far, so in the interest of continuous improvement, etc.).

BOX 1-10

Rejection Letter

BBB ORGANIZATION

Human Resources Department   P.O. Box 1234
Salaried Recruiting   St. Louis, MO 63130

Last Week's Date

Sue Smith
4321 Clark Road
St. Louis, MO 63130

Dear Sue:

Thank you for taking the time out of your schedule to discuss career opportunities with BBB Organization. The process of selection is always competitive. But based on my assessment of your skills, relative to those we need so badly, we are unable to extend to you an invitation to the next phase of our interview process.

Your resume and application is kept in our database for 6 months. Should an appropriate opportunity arise within another component, you will be contacted immediately by a representative of that component regarding your ability and interest.

Again, thank you for interviewing with us. We wish you success.

B. Jackson

Recruiting Specialist

Two people could role-play and debrief the conversation: discuss strengths, weaknesses, and potential for future personal issues. No two scenarios will be played out in exactly the same way. The power in this case lies in the students' creative ideas for approaching the director of human resources.

Appendix: A Few More Tips

The following pages contain miscellaneous information that you may find useful as you conceptualize, prepare, and deliver presentations.

CRITICAL SUCCESS FACTORS OF PRESENTATIONS

In addition to applying the five key elements of an effective presentation, there are some common sense rules used by most successful teams as they tell a story to an audience. Perhaps you'll see some new ideas here.

Prior to the Presentation:

Ask the client to summarize business issues into a one-sentence problem statement (also known as the "How to" question used to brainstorm solutions and ideas).

Prepare Concise Slides:

- List your team members' names (and the team/company name) on the title slide.
- Repeat the central idea as a footer on all slides.
- List a brief table of contents on a slide to provide the big picture of your presentation.
- Write either Q&A or your team's central idea on your final slide. This provides a simple visual background during questions.
- Distribute your slide copy (three slides to a page) before your presentation.

During the Presentation:

- Introduce all team members by name as you begin the presentation and as you transition between speakers.

- Stand, as a united team, to field questions during the Q&A.
- Maintain eye contact with each other to ensure that answers are organized.
- Control the timing of the presentation and Q&A. Your team leader should establish an out-of-time signal ahead of time.

Written Summary or Proposal:

- Write headings that are short and in the active voice.
- Pull readers through your prose by using bullets and enumerated points.
- Note your solution or major idea, and the benefits, clearly and early in the document.
- Distribute the executive summary or full proposal after your presentation and Q&A so that the audience can focus on what you say.

HOW TO PROVIDE CONSTRUCTIVE CRITICISM

Write in Behavioral Terms. In a written critique, use reader-based language. Write through the readers' eyes by tapping into their point of view (POV). Table 1-22 illustrates positive and negative written comments.

Speak in "I" Statements. In verbal critiques, the recipient often thinks about how to respond, and/or feels vulnerable about what you may say next. Your responsibility is to phrase your critique in the words and tone of voice that *you* would be comfortable receiving. Table 1-23 provides positive and negative examples.

TABLE 1-22   Written Critique

Positive Critique Example (notes exactly what to do differently)	Negative Critique Example (too vague)
Avoid these barriers to communication: your gestures did not match the importance of your topic, and your tone of voice was too flat for the exciting information you presented.	Communication barriers—gestures and tone of voice.

TABLE 1-23   Verbal Critique

Positive Critique Examples (positive, descriptive, and helpful)	Negative Critique Examples (too judgmental)
"I noticed that your left foot was moving during most of your presentation."	"You were too jumpy."
"In my opinion, greater voice inflection would make your topic more interesting."	"You weren't very interesting."
"I was unclear about the true intent of your objective."	"We didn't like that remark about your objective."
"I think you'd have incredible impact out in front of the podium and closer to the audience."	"You aren't tall enough to be behind the podium."
"I was distracted when you stood on one foot and then the other."	"Your embarrassment shows up in your weaving back and forth."

Bibliography

Brawer, R. A. (1998). *Fictions of Business: Insights on Management from Great Literature.* New York: John Wiley & Sons, Inc.

Conger, J. A. (1998). The Necessary art of persuasion. *Harvard Business Review*, May–June, 84–95.

Fielden, J. S. (1982). What do you mean you don't like my style? *Harvard Business Review*, May–June, 2–10.

Larkin, T. J., and Larkin, S. (1994). *Communicating Change: Winning Employee Support for New Business Goals.* New York: McGraw-Hill, Inc.

Munter, M. (2000). *Guide to Managerial Communication: Effective Business Writing* and *Speaking.* Upper Saddle River, NJ: Prentice Hall.

Quiñones, E. (1999, August 1). It was a dark and stormy sales pitch, and maybe it worked. *The New York Times*, 4.

Standard Oil Company of California (1949). *Correspondence Handbook.* California: Standard Oil Company of California.

Stewart, T. A. (1998). The cunning plots of leadership. *Fortune,* vol. 138, no. 5, September 7, 165–166.

Stockard, O. (1999). *The Write Approach: Techniques for Effective Business Writing.* San Diego: Academic Press.

The Oxford-Duden Pictorial English Dictionary (1995). New York: Oxford University Press.

2

Manager as Cross-Functional Leader of Diverse Teams

Introduction

Managers know that communication is a difficult, yet necessary part of the managerial role. Communicating with cross-functional teams is challenging because people come from many cultures, different disciplines, and varying perspectives. Communicating with direct reports requires great skill; communicating with nondirect reports presents interesting challenges.

Mark Rudloff is a marketing specialist manager with Patterson Dental Supply, Inc., located in St. Paul, Minnesota. Mr. Rudloff describes the challenge as follows, "Many successful organizations tend to run lean in size to cut overhead costs; this can lead to people overlooking critical communications outside of their immediate departments (out of sight, out of mind). We must have constant reminders to ensure that communication lines are not broken and factor in time for all parties to communicate with each other."

The cases in this chapter require the reader to consider many points of view. As in other chapters, the best learning occurs when readers discuss the cases because, of course, each reader brings a different perspective.

Example: Gathering Company-wide Perspectives

Do managers believe they know what their people think about the company, the culture, policies and procedures, and the managers? Some managers would probably say, "Yes, I believe that I have a pretty good handle on what people think around here."

Yet, do managers really know what their people think? In reality, no. We cannot read minds and we can be astounded to learn the deepest beliefs held by others. Multiply this reality by the number of divisions and departments in an organization and you perceive the difficult executive team task of "keeping a finger on the organization's pulse." It is true that companies have come a long way in surveying employee satisfaction: Savvy managers know they must collect the data, and more importantly, implement measurable changes that employees can see and feel. Employees perceive that if their "bottom-up" opinions result in "top-down" action, then managers truly *hear* their opinions. In other words, "my company cares enough about us to change something we targeted as needing improvement." Fortunate are the companies that have communications experts: those people skilled in gathering and synthesizing the diverse opinions of people from all organizational functions. Communications experts know how to take employee satisfaction several steps beyond the traditional survey process.

Ms. Joyce Serben, division VP, director corporate communications for Maritz® (world headquarters in Fenton, Missouri), ensures that employees have additional bottom-up communication vehicles. Ms. Serben has worked with Maritz management teams to implement three creative employee voice methods:

- Manager Gatekeepers
- Meet the Prez
- Online Town Hall Meetings

Manager Gatekeepers (referred to as such by this author for discussion in this casebook) is an effective method for gathering employee perceptions during times of change. The process comprises four steps. First, Ms. Serben, on an intermittent schedule (dictated by the scope and depth of a particular change initiative), asked a random number of senior- to middle-level managers to poll their people. Second, managers asked people to share their opinions and questions, as well as the rumors they'd heard, regarding a particular change initiative; managers also promised the employees anonymity. Third, managers called or e-mailed Ms. Serben with the latest employee perception trends. Fourth, Ms. Serben synthesized the information and shared it with senior executives. The management teams were then empowered with the necessary bottom-up information to respond to far-reaching concerns or wild rumors. Appropriate responses were built into senior executive speeches and department meeting materials.

This method obviously did not tap the opinions of every employee as a written survey would. The primary advantage of the Manager Gatekeeper method, however, is that managers realize real-time access to ever-evolving employee opinions and concerns. The secondary advantage is that senior- and middle-level managers engage in valuable conversations with employees, thus strengthening the trust between direct supervisors and direct reports. Larkin and Larkin (1994) suggest that the relationship between direct supervisors and employees is one that deserves strengthening because benefits such as increased trust are invaluable.

Meet the Prez is an effective method for minimizing the perceived gap between senior management and employees. The process involves a company-wide announcement, voluntary sign-ups, and an informal meeting with the president. First, Ms. Serben announced the Meet the Prez concept to the organization (e.g., via memo or e-mail). Second, interested employees placed their names on a list. No more than eight people were selected for the meeting; Ms. Serben selected names to represent a cross-section of the organization. Third, an informal meeting between the president and the select group of employees was held in the president's office. For people in jobs never requiring face-to-face visits to the president's office, this was a great opportunity to share ideas and get to know the person behind the title.

Online Town Hall Meetings were first initiated in Maritz Marketing Research, Inc. (MMRI) by the company's president, Tim Rogers, and vice president of marketing, Phil Wiseman. The MMRI meetings are labeled "Tim Talks." In the Maritz Performance Improvement Company (MPIC), the meetings are known as "Lipovsky Live," after MPIC's president, Ron Lipovsky. A third Maritz company, Maritz® Travel Company (MTC), calls its sessions the "MTC Superhighway." (Narsh, January/February 2000). The "MTC Superhighway" was later called "Reinberg Online," named after that company's leader.

The online sessions allow employees at headquarters and across field locations real-time access to the president via Intranet questions and answers. The process revolves around the categories in the company's employee satisfaction survey. Anyone can submit a question during a pre-established 90–minute period. Functional managers draft answers: e.g., the human resources VP might respond to questions related to salary. The president reviews the preliminary answers and composes final answers (then posted electronically) based on the management team's draft answer and the president's own viewpoint.

At MPIC, questions are received in real time and screened by the management team. Redundant questions are consolidated, questions aimed against individuals are screened out, and the few hostile questions are paraphrased or removed to an off-line list. A benefit of the Online Town Hall Meetings is that the rumor mill is stopped early. Another benefit is that people know they have access to the president on a relatively frequent basis.

CASES

Case 2-1   New Product Introduction

(Case purpose: Facilitate collaboration among departments.)

STEP 1: REVIEW THE BIG PICTURE

Assume that you are the owner of a family-owned and operated supply firm (you decide on the product line for this case); your company just passed from your father to you. You've waited for this chance to make some critical changes to processes and procedures because your father's hands-off approach resulted in many recurring problems. Your father retired, stating that he gave you complete control of the business. Your father never really controlled internal problems; he preferred to build consensus through many long conversations with department heads. Your opinion, however, is that strong leadership is needed—and now.

You have long worried about the working relationship between your marketing department and your purchasing department. The sales manager, once again, reminded you of the problem; she said "The new product just isn't available when we need it. Marketing advertises the heck out of it, but purchasing says they don't know anything about it. If you expect us to sell the stuff, you need to get marketing and purchasing on the same page. Now that you're in charge, fix this mess!"

You know the drill: you've seen enough references to it in your customer satisfaction data. Your company promotes new products; shortages appear when customers order the new products; overstocks of older, similar products result; and everybody is unhappy. The domino effect of unhappiness leads to much pointing of fingers and little generating of solutions:

- *Marketing* did what they were told: marketing created great promotions. "We create great advertising and then we don't see the revenue. No one understands how hard we work."
- *Purchasing* did what they were told: purchasing places orders upon direction. "We order when there is need or when you tell us to. When you don't speak up, we don't order. We get blamed because stock doesn't meet demand on new products—ones that you neglected to tell us would be promoted so heavily. We're just going by historical sales numbers on similar products. We didn't know to order such a large quantity of the new products."

- *Sales* did what they were told: salespeople promote new products. "You get us hyped up on new products and we're motivated to sell them. We win orders and then can't deliver. And guess who takes the heat from the customers? We do!"
- *Clients* did what they were told: they ordered new products because the supplier convinced them that the new products were better than the old. "I wonder why your company can't get its act together. You promote new products but can't deliver. And then you try to sell me the old product again! I can't meet my customers' needs if I don't know what I'll be using a week from now."

The same symptoms recur with no solution in sight. You feel caught in a trap like that old Abbot and Costello comedy routine, "Who's on First," but in your case, no one is on first. No one wins by the time the bases are rounded: everyone loses.

And, now, back to you, the *owner*. You've been asked to clean up the problem. You might like to say, "Play nice. Get the job done," but life isn't that easy: you cannot just issue a directive and walk away. You see that you have to own this problem and lead the generation of solutions. Your tasks are threefold:

1. *Preliminary fact-finding:* Identify the best method of communicating with all department heads regarding the issue (e.g., face-to-face, e-mail, voice mail, meeting, etc.).
2. *Generating ideas:* Identify the best method for documenting the root causes and solving the problem (e.g., which people will you consult; will you use a conversational meeting, a process flowchart, an affinity diagram, etc.?).
3. *Communicating final solution and next steps:* Identify the best method for communicating the final solution and next steps to your entire organization; describe how you will gain the buy-in of all relevant stakeholders.

STEP 2: ANALYZE FACTS AND EMOTIONS (F&Es)

If you analyze the facts versus the emotions of this case, it becomes clear that old problems need not only new solutions, but also new ways of viewing the problems. This is especially true given the fact that new leadership has just stepped in. If the new leader (the son of the original owner) does not make a difference now, he loses credibility at the beginning of his tenure—not a good proposition. See Table 2-1 for a sample analysis.

STEP 3: DESIGN THE STRATEGY

After analyzing the facts and emotions, it is clear that any number of approaches might work. The sample solution in this case assumes that the new owner is willing to risk alienating a few people because he truly believes that changing the culture and improving processes will result in enhanced customer satisfaction and increased revenues.

Begin with the old business adage, "what gets rewarded gets done," as a mental model for the solution to this case. Given that mental model, how do employees and managers know what gets rewarded? In most cases, job descriptions and performance evaluations list critical job competencies and everyone knows that, at minimum, these behaviors are expected.

TABLE 2-1 Analyze F&Es	
Facts (overview)	*Emotions (preliminary list)*
• The problem recurs and no one has yet implemented an answer. (Note: This does not mean that no one has thought of an answer! People seem to be waiting for someone else to lead the fray—the good old diffusion of responsibility theory at work again.) • People, as evidenced in their words and behaviors, are stuck in dealing with the symptoms, as opposed to taking action to look for solutions. • The timing of the new owner's response to this issue is critical: He can impact how his organization views him and he can quickly establish a new tone for his company's culture—a tone that indicates he will take charge and find answers, instead of continuing the old ways because "that's how we've always done it."	• The range of potential emotional issues might include: The previous owner (the father) says he'll stay out of it, but can we be sure of this if some employees run to him about the son's new ways? • The son has much to prove; will he push too hard to get the job done? • Some current department heads may resent the son's new style; they may feel that they are losing control. • Will people underestimate or overestimate the customers' responses? Will some people think "our clients haven't stopped ordering yet, so why worry about this?" Or will others think that the clients will jump ship tomorrow, so we'd better straighten up this minute? • Will people be ready to participate in a "new style" meeting using some technique like an affinity diagram or process flowcharting?

If the people representing the various groups in this company don't collaborate willingly, perhaps it is because there is no direct line of sight between that particular expected behavior and a reward. So, go to one of the original sources of the problem: go to the job description and performance evaluation documents, and edit them to reflect the necessary behaviors.

Mark Rudloff, marketing specialist manager with Patterson Dental Supply, Inc., says:

> If this occurred in my organization, a solution to the communication breakdown is first to rewrite job descriptions within my immediate marketing group to include communication and interaction with the purchasing department. Second, I'd make it a part of training early on for new employees, to teach them how essential this out-of-sight, out-of-mind function is. Third, I'd include various members of the marketing team in the regularly scheduled purchasing and marketing meetings. They can see first hand the issues that are present. It is also my hope that the people can get a feel for the processes involved with maintaining a tight inventory while providing the highest possible levels of customer service by having sufficient inventory levels of advertised products.

Mr. Rudloff's first idea went to the heart of the matter: One of the root causes starts with what we reward people for. Managers must clearly state behavioral expectations and create a means by which these behaviors get rewarded, before expecting people in different groups, focused on different functions, to see the invisible need for such behaviors.

Mr. Rudloff's second idea went to the point-of-view issue inherent in so many cross-functional difficulties: Emotionally, people cannot or will not understand another point of view until they "see" it. This often means that managers must literally *cross-pollinate* their regular department meetings and problem-solving sessions with key personnel from the other departments. Some managers use temporary assignments for just this purpose: to exchange the points of view between two collaborative groups.

Case 2-2   Maximizing the Communications Function

(Case purpose: Sell the benefits of a formal communications function in your company.)

STEP 1: REVIEW THE BIG PICTURE

In this case, you are on a cross-functional senior management team in a multinational service-based corporation; your group represents the key functions in your organization (e.g., operations, human resources, marketing, sales, training and development, and customer relations). You believe that it is time for your corporation to install a corporate communications vice president and staff. Executive management is open to the idea; however, they are concerned about the cost of the new department and they view the corporate communications function as similar to freelance writing. A recent statement by the CEO sums up this view: "We'll finalize our strategies first, then we'll call in this new VP of communications to write it up for our employees. I just don't see how a communications expert can help us strategize."

Your cross-functional team is to prepare a high-level strategic plan presentation to sell the new communications function to executives. Your first step is to brainstorm *driving forces* and *restraining forces*, so that you can use this information to develop a strategy. For example, you must persuade the executives that the new function is a value-added, necessary idea; the tougher sell, however, is that you must convince executives that the VP of communications needs early access to their planning meetings.

A team member suggests using a traditional T chart for a force field analysis. He notes that your team can use the resulting ideas during your strategic plan presentation in the following ways:

- "We can position *driving forces* in the benefits statements during our presentation. For example, we need to agree with the executives about things that don't need change. Because we expect resistance, we must find points about which to agree. I think we'll more effectively persuade them by establishing common ground."
- "We can translate any *restraining forces* into clear, simple solutions. For example, for every barrier that we expect them to throw out, let's create a solution. We

already know that they prefer to hear about issues for which there are solutions. Let's persuade them by providing simple solutions."

Your task is twofold: First, *brainstorm*, using a force field analysis, the driving forces, and restraining forces related to this problem statement: "Why should our organization build a formal corporate-wide communications function (with VP and related staff)?" Second, *outline your basic ideas* for the flow of your strategic plan presentation. For example, using the *Presentation Standards* (originally discussed in Chapter 1 of this casebook), outline what your team will present for the five elements of your presentation:

1. Introduction and central idea
2. Purpose and executive objectives
3. Big picture
4. Logical content flow supported by evidence
5. Conclusion

STEP 2: ANALYZE FACTS AND EMOTIONS (F&Es)

First, *brainstorm* what executives like about the formal corporate-wide communications function and list what you perceive as their concerns. Next, *rate* the driving forces and restraining forces to identify where your team should spend the most presentation time and persuasive effort (see the sample T chart in Table 2-2).

STEP 3: DESIGN THE STRATEGY

Now, use the *Fast Start to Preparing a Presentation* (first discussed in Chapter 1 of this casebook) to outline preliminary ideas for presenting your high-level strategic plan (see the sample in Table 2-3).

TABLE 2-2 Sample T Chart

Instructions:
- List driving forces in left column and list restraining forces in right column.
- Rate each *driving force* as follows (to assess presentation time and persuasive effort):
  3 = Most powerful/useful for our strategic plan
  2 = Somewhat powerful/useful for our strategic plan
  1 = Least powerful/useful for our strategic plan
- Rate each *restraining force* as follows (to assess presentation time and persuasive effort):
  3 = Greatest barrier to our strategic plan
  2 = Somewhat of a barrier to our strategic plan
  1 = Least of the barriers to our strategic plan

Driving Forces "+"	3	2	1	Restraining Forces "−"	3	2	1
(e.g., people, factors, perceptions that support the change)				(e.g., people, factors, perceptions that may prohibit/resist change)			
Division heads communicated differently to groups recently. The miscommunication was a case in point for why we need a formal function.	3			Executives aren't convinced that the value added from communications function will offset the costs.	3		
The CEO offered, at least, conceptual support for the idea.		2		A few executives like the "closed club;" they may fear communications VP intrusion.	3		
The most recent employee satisfaction survey showed that employees at locations other than headquarters feel left out of the loop.	3			Some executives may ignore suggestions from communications VP because "we know strategy" and "you know how to write."		2	
Etc. (your ideas here. . .)				Etc. (your ideas here. . .)			

TABLE 2-3   Fast Start to Preparing a Presentation

Five Key Elements	*Presentation Outline (bulleted ideas)*
I. Introduction and Central Idea	**Introduction:** Quick story about consequences of miscommunications among divisions at another multinational company. (Potential benefit of this strategy: Executives relate to the story without becoming defensive about their own recent conflicting communications.)
	Central idea: "Common Communication, Uncommon Customer Satisfaction" (Potential benefit of this strategy: Executives may be less concerned about happy employees than they are happy customers and, therefore, solid revenues. This draws a direct line of sight between executive and manager communications, employee satisfaction, and customer satisfaction.)
II. Our Purpose Versus Executives' Objectives	**Our Purpose:** To convince you (the executives) that the benefits of a formal communications function outweigh the costs.
	Executives' Objectives: • You'll streamline corporate-wide communications, thereby freeing executive meeting time for strategic planning. • You'll delegate critical communication tasks, thereby freeing your valuable time. • You'll clarify the company's vision, mission, policies, and procedures for employees (through formal function), thereby creating more company consistency in the eyes of our customers.
III. Big Picture (Table of Contents)	**Today, we'll talk about:** • Why we need the formal communications function. • How other companies effectively utilize the function. • What we need to do to initiate the function, and when. • Who will own the start-up of the function—and timelines?
IV. Logical Content Flow With Evidence	(Follow the flow of the big picture here and include relevant statistics and examples. Details TBD.)
V. Conclusion	• Repeat benefits (in terms of executives' objectives) here. • Repeat central idea: "Common Communication, Uncommon Customer Satisfaction." • Q&A.

Case 2-3   Policy Rollout Plan
(Case purpose: Decide how to communicate a new policy.)

STEP 1: REVIEW THE BIG PICTURE

Assume that you are the human resources director for a national organization (world headquarters in Cincinnati, with field offices and plants distributed throughout the United States). The executive committee, in collaboration with your office and the legal department, just approved a new policy and procedures related to "comp days" (i.e., earning compensation hours for overtime worked). You disseminated the terms of the new comp days policy via memo to all managers and employees.

Within 1 week of the memo distribution, you began receiving phone calls and e-mails from managers and employees. You've been frustrated with many of the questions because you believe that you described relevant details in your memo.

However, a manager illuminated another point of view when she said, "Think of it this way. Who had a *need to know what, and when*? We, as managers, needed to thoroughly understand the new policy before our people showed up at our doorsteps with a million questions. Now we look stupid in front of our people—and headquarters looks like it doesn't know how to communicate."

Your task: If you had it all to do over again, how would you rollout the communication of the new comp days policy to the organization? Organize a sequential list of steps as your new rollout plan.

STEP 2: ANALYZE FACTS AND EMOTIONS (F&Es)

Facts and Emotions

Yes, managers are funny that way: They like to know about official policies before the rest of the organization! This is based on emotion, yes; but there is a sound factual reason behind why managers need to know first. Managers and direct line supervisors rely on their credibility to garner and maintain the trust of the people in their departments. If they seem not to be "in the know" once too often, employees will begin to discount the importance of their managers and supervisors, and managers viewed as unimportant or uninformed will soon be avoided or misjudged.

It is senior management's responsibility to see that their management team is well informed, not only with the facts but also with the tools to implement those facts with their people. In this case, *when* different groups received the information is only one issue. A second issue is *how* the information will be used: Managers needed tools and peripheral materials.

STEP 3: DESIGN THE STRATEGY

Table 2-4 provides a possible set of steps for the rollout of the comp days policy change.

TABLE 2-4   Strategy for Comp Days Rollout

Step Number	Activity

Step 1	• Finalize comp days policy with legal and executive management.
	• Write memo to managers, to accompany new policy page (to replace page XX in Policies and Procedures Manual).
	• Conduct session with cross-section of managers and direct line supervisors:
	  1. Obtain their feedback about wording of memo to managers.
	  2. Document their questions about how to implement the new policy.
	  3. Ask them for special case scenarios that have arisen in the past or that might arise in the future.

Step 2	Translate results of session with managers and supervisors into the following peripheral materials: • Frequently asked questions (FAQs) and answers. • Steps to follow in the event of a special case.
Step 3	Distribute memo to managers with these items attached: • New comp plan policy page (with instructions to replace page XX in Policies and Procedures Manual) • Suggested agenda to use during meeting with employees • FAQs • Sample special cases • Steps to follow in the event of a special case
Step 4	Distribute a different memo to all employees (1 week after distributing the memo to managers). Direct employees to supervisors with questions.

Case 2-4   Retail Redesign

(Case purpose: Address retail salespersons' issues while adhering to franchise rules.)

STEP 1: REVIEW THE BIG PICTURE

For the purposes of this case, you are one of three managers at a retail outlet in a large suburban shopping mall; your franchise store exclusively represents the educational products and toys of an international manufacturer. The manufacturer also introduced a line of children's clothing 12 months ago. The retail stores of this corporation, across all international locations, are recognized among consumers as having consistent store format and displays, superior customer service, outstanding merchandise quality, and simple return policies.

The franchise stores are known, across the retail industry, for maintaining loyal and frequent customers. Customer satisfaction, on a 7–point scale, has consistently rated 6.6 and above for the past 5 years (e.g., on items such as salesperson friendliness, merchandise quality, neatness and cleanliness of store, and ease of merchandise return).

When you first arrived at your retail store 2 years ago, however, you inherited a sales staff lacking in customer handling skills and salespeople preferring to wait for you to direct them on tasks large and small. After many weeks of training, coaching, and performance ratings and discussions, you finally elevated the staff's behavior. Your salespeople now receive customer satisfaction ratings consistent with the average ratings across all franchises, and they independently solve problems. During this 2-year period, you terminated the employment of only one employee. You now pride yourself on the level of self-empowerment among employees.

Four months ago, a manager left your store because his spouse transferred to another geographic region of the United States. A new manager transferred in to your location; your retail outlet has a total of three managers: you, another seasoned manager at your location (Jack), and the new manager (Audrey). Audrey, after her tenure in your store, is slated for promotion to regional management.

During the last 4 months, you and Jack have noticed a distinct pattern evolving among your salespeople. When you or Jack request special assistance (e.g., working late, working on a Saturday if someone else cannot make it, helping with unforeseen merchandise rearrangements), the employees remain helpful. When Audrey asks for assistance, the employees have many reasons precluding their cooperation. The employees dubbed Audrey the "company gal" (behind her back, of course) because Audrey follows the franchise policies and procedures to the letter. You and Jack follow the rules but allow a bit more flexibility.

In addition, the corporate office announced, 6 months ago, a massive overhaul of its franchise retail outlets to include redesigned store layouts; new, high-tech point-of-purchase displays; and a new line of computer-based educational products requiring hands-on computer demonstration desks in the stores.

Renovation began quickly at your store and the contractors finished within the expected deadline. Even though the chaos of renovation affected your customer traffic and complicated the work flow in your store, most salespeople demonstrated positive behaviors through what they said and did. Customers often express pleasure regarding the new store layout and adults seem to enjoy testing software in the store before purchasing and installing it in their homes for children.

Four weeks ago, however, the corporate office announced employee policies and procedures that increasingly impact the relationships between the managers and the employees, the reaction of the salespeople to their work, and the perceptions of customers about their in-store experiences.

You, along with the other managers, received well-written guidelines and instructions about the new requirements. Each of you read the manager preparation package in your free time at home. Three weeks ago you implemented the new procedures with your employees. This is the point at which the real issues began.

The new employee policies and procedures include (but are not limited to) the items in Table 2-5.

You and the other two managers have heard many employee complaints including:

- "They don't trust us now! Why?"
- "I'm being treated like a new employee. I don't look forward to coming to work."
- "Four regular customers complained to me last week about how messy the store looks lately, and I can't clean it up until a manager tells me to do it! Plus, I'm staying

TABLE 2-5   Policy Changes

Previous Policies and Procedures (Were in place for 5 years)	New Policies and Procedures (Implemented 3 weeks ago)
Employees, when not helping customers, will process returns and return the merchandise to the shelves.	Managers will direct employees to process returns at designated time of day.
Employees will straighten shelves whenever they see the need (to maintain franchise standards for neatness).	Managers will direct employees to straighten shelves when the manager sees the need.
Employees will clean the store daily (to maintain franchise standards for cleanliness).	Managers will delegate the cleaning of the store prior to the first shift on Monday mornings.
Employees will receive written performance reviews every quarter from their managers.	Managers will write and deliver to the employee a written performance evaluation at the end of each work shift, every day of work

late now just to process these returns when I could've done it at spots during the day when we didn't have customers."

- "Audrey wrote me up for not waiting for her to tell me what to do! If I see a shirt that needs folding and no customers are in the store, why do I have to wait to be told what to do?"

You and Jack have continued to allow your employees freedom of choice in completing tasks; however, you have completed the performance evaluations after each shift. Audrey, on the other hand, follows the letter of the new policies.

Your task is to answer the following questions:

1. What are the root causes of the issues at your retail outlet?
2. Is there room for managerial freedom beyond the new rules?
3. What can you, as a manager group of three, do to solve the problems?

STEP 2: ANALYZE FACTS AND EMOTIONS (F&Es)

This case requires analyzing the points of view of several stakeholders. We start with the customer because, ultimately, the bottom line is related to customer satisfaction. Review Table 2-6 and add information as needed.

STEP 3: DESIGN THE STRATEGY

Your task was to answer the following questions: (1) What are the root causes of the issues at your retail outlet? (2) Is there room for managerial freedom, beyond the new franchise rules? (3) What can you, as a manager group of three, do to solve the problems?

First, the *root causes*, as explored in Step 2 of this case, are:

- Different managers behave inconsistently with the employees in this store.
- The new policies reduced the previous level of employee empowerment.

TABLE 2-6 Analysis of F&Es

Stakeholder	Emotional Perceptions and Factual Behaviors	A Real Reason Behind the Emotions and the Facts
Customer	**Emotion:** Something feels different (e.g., the store looks messier than normal, the salespeople seem less happy). **Factual Behavior:** Since I don't feel as special in here as I once did, I may shop elsewhere more often.	Employees lost their empowerment (i.e., reasonable freedom and appropriate control) and let their negative feelings show with customers.
Salespersons	**Emotion:** I can't think for myself now. I'm evaluated every time I turn around! **Factual Behavior:** I wait for managers to tell me what to do.	Employees lost empowerment and managers now dictate even simple tasks.
Managers 1 and 2: You and Jack	**Emotion:** The corporate rules have gone too far. **Factual Behavior:** I'll use my judgment about when to apply the letter of the law.	Managers are now told to dictate tasks that we've worked hard to empower our salespeople to do naturally.
Manager 3: Audrey	**Emotion:** The corporate rules are the corporate rules. If I follow them, then I'll get that regional promotion. **Factual Behavior:** I'll follow the rules as they're written.	Managers are responsible for everything in our stores.

Second, *managerial freedom* depends on the individual manager's perception of the rules and the behavior resulting from these perceptions. Gail T. Fairhurst and Robert A. Sarr, in their book entitled *The Art of Framing: Managing the Language of Leadership*, note that "Mental models of how the world works (or is supposed to work) help us to size up situations and formulate our goals for communicating" (p. 23).

Audrey's mental model of her managerial world is clearly "follow the rules and I will move forward." Your mental model, as well as Jack's mental model, is probably more along the lines of "follow the rules that make sense and use my sound managerial judgment on the others." The differing managerial styles aggravate employees; employees, in turn, treat the managers differently (i.e., helping you and Jack; avoiding assistance to Audrey). Managers and employees perceive and respond based on their mental models of how their retail outlet is supposed to work.

The first task for the management team of three is to *agree to support* a more similar list of managerial behaviors. This may take several meetings. Are there risks in this effort? Yes, there are risks. If Audrey takes the company gal approach too far, she could report you and Jack for not following procedures. You would have to judge this risk given the real context. However, some managerial freedom (i.e., sound judgment) may need to be exercised when applying the new rules.

Third, the management team, to solve the problem, must help all managers *and* employees envision a mutual picture—a mental model—of what successfully operating their retail outlet comprises. This endeavor may require a couple of meetings to define what is acceptable and what is not, while appropriately adhering to the corporate rules. If the rules are discussed, in tandem with contextual examples of how to logically apply the rules, then everyone has a better chance of working together.

If the rules unreasonably control the staff, then valued employees may decide to work elsewhere. What if valued employees are replaced by people who wait to be told what steps to take? Then might customers leave their discomfort at this retail outlet and shop elsewhere?

Case 2-5   Performance Evaluation Dilemma

(Case purpose: Handle a difficult employee performance evaluation.)

STEP 1: REVIEW THE BIG PICTURE

Assume that you are a manager of a work group totaling 17 people (i.e., degreed professionals, administrative personnel, and technical support experts). You were promoted, from a different department, into this job 9 months ago. Performance evaluations in your organizations occur annually. You have conducted all but one performance evaluation: the one you assume will be the most difficult.

The last performance evaluation meeting is with one of your degreed professionals (let's call this person D); you experienced numerous issues with D over the past several months. When you checked D's previous evaluations for the past 3 years (written by the former manager), you could find little documentation regarding any negative work behavior. In fact, the ratings were consistently in the average to above-average range. You found only a single negative reference in an evaluation from 2 years ago: "D's attitude seems to occasionally interfere with productivity."

The recent problems with D include behaviors such as the following: recurring late arrivals to work, project budget overruns, and disagreements with peers and the administrative support people. You tried to document specific examples of these problems in the current performance evaluation; however, you did not maintain a weekly file of D's work behaviors. Thus, you worry about defending the low rating.

Your performance evaluation meeting with D progresses as follows outlined in Table 2-7.

Your task is to analyze the situation and strategize how to proceed with the evaluation.

TABLE 2-7 Interview with D

You: "Hello, D. How are you today?" (D shakes your hand and remains silent.) "Well, as you know, we're here to discuss your performance evaluation today. Before we review the evaluation I've written, how do you think your year has gone?"

D: "Fine. I consistently get great results from my projects and the clients are always happy in the end."

You: "And how do you think you've fared within the department?"

D: "I'm a team player. No problems. I do have some issues with Lana, but we just keep hammering away at them. We have different professional views about how to run projects."

You: "I think my evaluation ratings and comments are somewhat different from your perceptions. Let me explain your evaluation and then let's discuss the situation. First, I think you have excellent technical skills; quality issues never seem to arise in your projects. Second, I believe we have problems in three areas: you often arrive late to work, your projects often incur budget overruns, and there seem to be disagreements with several of your peers and the administrative support people. However, with your strong technical expertise and tenure, I believe we can work out these three issues. We have talked about them before, as you probably recall." (At this point, you show D the specific ratings on the performance evaluation form.)

D: "I'm not going to sign this. No way. I'm not the problem. I come in late because I work late. The cost overruns are never my fault; something unexpected always comes up. And, I'm not taking the flack for personality conflicts. Lana, for example, is hard to get along with. I know you agree. Who is saying all of this stuff? Give me names."

You: "We're here to talk about you. D, do you think . . . "

D: "I do more work than Lana. I'm easier to get along with. And I heard that her performance evaluation went just fine! Why is her evaluation great and mine is not?" (You're surprised: Her evaluation was better. However, you did not discuss these confidential reviews with other employees.)

STEP 2: ANALYZE FACTS AND EMOTIONS (F&Es)

Analyze the points listed in Table 2-8.

STEP 3: DESIGN THE STRATEGY

Review the ideas listed in Table 2-9. What recommendations might you add to this manager's strategic plan? (See the "Coaching Techniques" in Chapter 7).

FREQUENTLY ASKED QUESTIONS: ASK AN ATTORNEY

If you ask managers about their favorite task, few would say that they most enjoy conducting performance evaluations of employees. Managers serious about their coaching role understand the importance of conducting thorough and honest performance evaluations.

Managers afraid of confrontation with their employees, however, may help create some of the long-standing performance problems. For example, consider an all too common example. An employee demonstrates marginal job performance and yet the

TABLE 2-8   Analysis of F&Es

The Facts	The Emotions
You lack adequate supporting documentation (i.e., you did not maintain a file on your employees).	**Yours:** You feel unprepared if D disagrees with your ratings. You perceive that you are at a disadvantage.
	D's: D picked up clues about your managerial style during the informal performance discussions to date. If D perceives that you haven't maintained good records, then D may feel an advantage.
You delayed the most difficult evaluation.	**Yours:** You're nervous.
	D's: D is aggravated that you scheduled D's meeting until last. D has used that time to gather what information she or he could from at least one other person about the evaluations.
D's opinions and your opinions are far apart.	**Yours:** You feel like it is a matter of "he said, she said." You wish you'd kept better records.
	D's: D will continue to ask for names and disagree about specific examples (i.e., there is always a good reason for my behavior).
D jumped to defending and challenging your evaluation ratings and comments. D skipped the step of asking "Why?"	**Yours:** You feel attacked. You knew this would happen.
	D's: D feels angry.

manager rates her as "satisfactory" on her annual performance evaluation. What happens to this employee when a new manager assumes leadership of the department? What happens when this new manager *is* willing to match written performance ratings to the employee's actual performance and a series of "not satisfactory" ratings appear on the performance evaluation?

Most likely, the employee reacts negatively and a difficult conversation ensues. The new manager is frustrated, the employee is confused and angry, and the resulting communications are unnecessarily complicated by the former manager's lack of truthful performance ratings.

The paper trail of documentation remaining from the former manager's files only serves to hurt the new manager's attempts to coach the employee's performance up to standard. In worst case scenarios, this paper trail seems to prove the opposite if the new manager must finally terminate the employee for performance issues.

Managers frequently have questions about how to write and communicate accurate and honest performance evaluations. The questions and answers in Table 2-10 reflect some of the more frequent of these issues.

The author thanks Mr. Dan O'Toole, an attorney with the law firm of Armstrong Teasdale, LLP, located in St. Louis, Missouri, for his input into the following questions and answers. Mr. O'Toole specializes in employment law, representing corporations.

TABLE 2-9 Design the Strategy

Before Your Meeting	Review previous project documents to jog your memory about critical dates related to D's work performance (month/year dates are better than vague references). List positive and negative examples of D's work.
	Question clients and other managers (on a need to know basis) to document their statements about D's work performance. Ask for specific examples of what D *says* and *does*—avoid statements about attitude.
During Your Meeting	Use the common *sandwich* technique (this was reflected in the previous conversation): List positive examples first, then list areas needing improvement, and end on a positive note.
	Refuse to discuss another employee's performance in D's performance evaluation meeting. Managers risk lawsuits when they discuss confidential performance issues with other employees.
	Maintain a calm demeanor; do not respond to any emotional displays with similar displays or unprofessional words or behaviors.
	Focus on the trends reflected in D's behaviors: Try sketching a picture to illustrate this to D. For example, draw a simple *core competency illustration* in the shape of a bull's eye. List key evaluation items in the center. Then reflect D's actual work behaviors by placing dots on the drawing (i.e., positive ratings are dots within the bull's eye, and negative ratings are dots outside the target).
	Ask D probing *why* and *how* questions. You must learn how D perceives work and people, and you must understand how D solves problems on the job. Then you are better prepared to coach D.
At the Conclusion of Your Meeting	Refer again to your illustration.
	State, and write, the critical behavior changes required of D. Clarify the benefits of such changes for D, for the department, and for the clients.
	Emphasize that D controls the choice to change behaviors.
	Ask D to reiterate performance expectations. Clarify where necessary.
	Set a follow-up meeting.

TABLE 2-10   Frequently Asked Questions

Q   I've overheard a few managers talking at lunch about their problem employees. Some of what they say is quite negative and occasionally the jokes made about the employees are quite negative. What is the recommended policy about this kind of behavior?

A   Managers should share information about an employee's performance with another manager on a need to know basis. For example, if an employee is assigned to a cross-functional team, that person's manager may have reason to discuss performance behaviors with the other manager. However, derogatory conversations serve no purpose other than gossip and are perceived simply as bad business.

Q   I completed new supervisor training last week. The trainer criticized my answer to one of the exercises. I'd written the following sentence as part of a sample performance evaluation comment: "Lola's attitude regarding her work seems to be negative." I took special care to word it as "seems to be negative" as opposed to "is negative." What's the problem here?

A   First, "seems to be" is indeed softer and less emphatic language than "is." However, the problem rests in the word "attitude." You cannot document Lola's *attitude* because attitude resides within a person's private thoughts. By contrast, you can document *behavior* because behavior may be identified and measured by observing what a person says and does. Second, limit your descriptions to observable and measurable comments and avoid assumptions.

Poor example: "Lola comes in late to work too often. Apparently she does not see the importance of arriving on time."

Better example: "Lola arrives late to work, on average, 3 days each week. I have discussed the importance of arriving to work on time with Lola on 3 separate occasions, over the course of 3 weeks."

From a legal point of view, when you document performance issues, it is best to use objective, not subjective, descriptions. Objective descriptions serve as better evidence. Also, consider the time lag that occurs between writing a performance evaluation and responding to a lawsuit that may be filed later. It simply helps your recall to read objective descriptions.

Q   Must I wait for the annual performance evaluation to document an employee's performance?

A   Document an employee's performance throughout the year. Maintain a file on each employee: list dates, positive and negative behaviors and events, and the consequences of those behaviors and events (e.g., a "drop file"). Discuss your expectations with the employee on an ongoing basis. Tell the employee when he or she does well and when performance needs improvement. Ongoing discussions and documentation are the keys to legally defensible documentation: There should be no surprises in a performance evaluation. These suggestions are simply components of fairness: Any employer would want to be in a position of fairness.

Q   Is it safe for me to discuss television shows or books, relating to gender or racial differences, with my coworkers?

A   The best policy is to avoid these discussions. An innocent conversation or comment could later be drawn into evidence during a lawsuit.

Q   Should I keep my division head informed of a problem employee's performance by sending him e-mails?

A   It is a good idea to keep your direct line supervisor informed. However, in the event of a lawsuit by your employee, your entire e-mail system can become part of a discovery request. People tend to be less formal in e-mail discussions and things written can be taken out of context. You may wish to update your supervisor via verbal communications and written memos.

Q   Is it wrong to use simple phrases that are often part of informal conversations, like "You can't teach an old dog new tricks?"

TABLE 2-10   *(continued)*

A	The best policy is to avoid these phrases entirely. These comments can be used as evidence of age discrimination, for example. Avoid comments about age, gender, religion, national origin, or disability status.
Q	If I say something to an employee and there is no witness, can my statement be used in court?
A	Yes, what you say can be included as evidence.
Q	I'm worried about how my employee will handle a poor performance evaluation. I'm afraid that I'll never get any good work out of that person. Isn't it better to just give middle-of-the-road performance ratings on evaluations?
A	Managers sometimes avoid targeting below-standard behaviors and honestly discussing these performance issues with employees. However, this is a bad strategy. If and when that employee must be terminated, the documentation left behind in these performance evaluations only serves to hurt the manager and company. If you give good ratings that are undeserved, then you must disprove your own documentation if you terminate an employee and she or he files a lawsuit. Remember, there should be no surprises: use appropriate progressive discipline.
Q	I handled a difficult performance evaluation meeting the other day. The employee was unhappy with the ratings I'd given her. During our meeting, she wanted to talk about another employee's performance. I refused to discuss the other employee with her. Did I do the right thing?
A	Yes. The focus of your meeting was to evaluate the performance of one employee. You were correct in not discussing another employee's performance: confidentiality is a must.
Q	We had to fire a person this week. What do we tell the client who was used to dealing with that person?
A	You should not discuss specifics with the client. Simply say that the person is no longer with your firm and, of course, handle the transition of project-related tasks as you would in any other job change situation. If you talk about why the person left the company, which is essentially publication to a third party outsider, it could potentially be proven as defamation. You may or may not be able to prove the truthfulness of what you've said about the person.
Q	Can a document or report, generated for our company by a consultant, be used in a lawsuit against us?
A	Yes, the document can be used as evidence in a lawsuit. Ensure that documents avoid verbiage that could be construed as biased.
Q	How do I instruct people in my department about how to handle politically incorrect e-mails?
A	Employees should learn the legalities of using company-based e-mail systems. Tell people to refrain from sending such e-mails. You should also tell people to delete such e-mails and avoid forwarding them. Employers should create policies about e-mail and Internet usage.

Bibliography

Fairhurst, G. T., and Sarr, R. A. (1996). *The Art of Framing: Managing the Language of Leadership.* San Francisco: Jossey-Bass Publishers.

Larkin, T. J., and Larkin, S. (1994). *Communicating Change: Winning Employee Support for New Business Goals.* New York: McGraw-Hill, Inc.

Narsh, R. (2000). The town hall meeting for the next century. *Journal of Communication Manager*, January/February.

3

Manager as Idea Generator

We need new ideas.
So, we need to ask different questions.

Introduction

Managers of any tenure have probably experienced the frustration of trying to find new solutions to long-standing problems. Sometimes employees wait for the manager to propose the answer, at other times a lone employee has an answer that goes unsupported by his peers.

Perhaps the traditional hierarchical structure inherent in many organizations limits the exploration of new ideas. Because of this structure, perhaps the questions asked—and how they are asked—limit the range and quality of the answers we get. And, lest we forget, the very nature of specialized work groups inhibits people from thinking in big picture terms and leads them to limited points of view. Gareth Morgan, author of *Images of Organization*, notes (on p. 29) that:

These problems are often compounded by the fact that mechanistic definitions of job responsibilities encourage many organizational members to adopt mindless, unquestioning attitudes such as "it's not my job to worry about that," " that's his responsibility, not mine," or "I'm here to do what I'm told."

The cases in this chapter ask readers an important question: "How can we explore issues to discover creative solutions *and* get the best thinking from the most people?" Each case represents an opportunity to look at familiar issues with new eyes, and offers readers a point of discussion from which to share their perspectives and ideas. The responsibility of the manager is less focused on knowing the answer; the responsibility of the manager, by contrast, is more focused on finding group facilitation methodologies that will allow people to discover the most feasible answers.

CASES

Case 3-1   Establishing Values in a New Team

(Case purpose: Synthesize opinions among new team members.)

STEP 1: REVIEW THE BIG PICTURE

First, this case causes you to think beyond the traditional *icebreaker* activities when forming new teams. Typical icebreaker exercises work well within the confines of their purpose: to facilitate people getting to know each other. However, many teams rapidly experience project pressures that test their flexibility and resilience; team members must not only know each other quickly, they must establish effective communication strategies and they must design efficient work-flow patterns.

Second, this case requires that you follow a flow of logic from *opinions*, to *values*, to *behaviors*. Successful fast track teams move beyond the *getting to know you* phase and quickly establish common values and behaviors—based on blended individual opinions and values. The SWOT Analysis (recommended in this case) is used in Chapter 7 for a team in crisis; please consider it as a proactive tool *while forming* teams. Also, to facilitate team agreement regarding values and behaviors, the team must define what comprises *acceptable team behavior*. The behaviorally anchored rating scale (BARS) is a method recommended to help teams think along a continuum: my opinions, my values, our values, our acceptable team behaviors.

Background

Assume that, as an executive in charge of a multinational project, you assembled three of your organization's brightest people into a cross-functional team. Your team, during the course of a 9-month project timeline, will work at different client locations (two cities in Japan and one city in the state of California).

You scheduled 6 hours, tomorrow, for your team's project orientation session. At 6:45 P.M. tomorrow evening, everyone boards a flight for the client headquarters; your group must, literally overnight, *feel and function* like a team. During the orientation session, you intend to ask people to introduce themselves and summarize their areas of expertise. You then plan to explain the project scope and timelines, team member roles and responsibilities, and your leadership function. You'll close by describing the client situation, client roles and responsibilities, and any key features that make this project dissimilar to other projects.

You believe you have a solid team orientation session until a colleague, over lunch today, suggests that you ask your new team to conduct a SWOT analysis of themselves and their newly formed team. You asked your friend about the timing of this tactic (you normally use a SWOT analysis during a project crisis).

She responded, "Your team hits the ground running in 2 days—in front of your key clients' eyes and ears. If I were you, I'd make sure that my team established a common vision of our *values and acceptable behaviors*, not just our roles and responsibilities, before going on location with clients. I learned this the hard way, believe me! I believe that intense project teams can be like new relationships. The road is too rocky and the work twice as hard if members don't agree to value the same things during the course of the working relationship. So, ask your people to run a SWOT analysis of their team now, before you get into the heat of the project."

Your Tasks

You walk away from lunch convinced that your colleague is right. Your task is as follows:

1. **Decide when to facilitate the SWOT analysis.** First, decide *when* to facilitate the SWOT analysis (e.g., beginning, middle, or end of the team orientation session).
2. **Complete a SWOT analysis chart.** Second, simulate a SWOT analysis for a hypothetical team (see Table 3-1 in "Step #2: Analyze Facts and Emotions" in this case) or for a small team within your classroom. People first write their own ideas in silence before the next discussion step occurs.
3. **Analyze the *why behind people's opinions*.** Third, discuss *individuals' perspectives, opinions, and values*, as illuminated in their respective SWOT analysis charts.
4. **Agree on a list of team values.** Fourth, agree on a list of *team values* (i.e., team members agree to support the values for the duration of the project; complete consensus is not necessary).
5. **Transform team values into acceptable team behaviors.** Fifth, use the BARS technique to translate team values into *acceptable team behaviors* (see "Step #3: Design the Strategy" in this case).

Individuals or small teams may work on these tasks. Individuals may work through the sample solution for this case. Small teams may use the sample solution as a guide and then simulate the recommended SWOT analysis for their work team.

STEP 2: ANALYZE FACTS AND EMOTIONS (F&Es)

First, decide when to facilitate the SWOT analysis. Ask: What do team members need to know about the project (the *what, when, where, why*), about each other (the *who*), and about working together (the *how*)? Therefore, when will I schedule the SWOT analysis (i.e., beginning, middle, or end of the team orientation session)?

Second, complete a SWOT analysis chart. Brainstorm the kind of information that you might gather for each person from a typical team, using the four columns of a SWOT analysis chart. Each person completes the chart silently on paper, then the team documents ideas and discusses them.

- If you work alone on this case, review Table 3-1 (SWOT Analysis Chart for a Hypothetical Three-Person Team).
- If a small team in a classroom works on this case, brainstorm from respective individual team member perspectives.

TABLE 3-1	SWOT Analysis Chart for a Hypothetical Three-Person Team			

Team Member	Strengths (this is true of me/be specific)	Weaknesses (this is true of me/be specific)	Opportunities (our team has the chance to really. . .)	Threats (things that could block our team's success are . . .)
Clark	• Financial skills. • Intervention during interpersonal disagreements. • I can "read the client" (e.g., clients say that I understand what they want).	• Weak grammar skills. • When timelines are tight, I focus on tasks and forget to show consideration for others.	• We're smart: we can efficiently complete tasks. • We're on the same team: we'll argue infrequently. • We're fast: we'll get to sleep at reasonable hours.	• I know this client demands unreasonable deadlines. • The people on our team have different opinions about final report style.
Chris	• Writing skills. • Presentation skills. • I stay completely focused on tasks until finished; I expect others to do the same.	• Computational skills. • "People problems" annoy me.	• Our visibility with senior management is great on this project; if we succeed, we're up for promotions. • Chance to return to client for more work in the future.	• There could be too much work for just three people and one director.
Felicity	• Data analysis. • Financial skills.	• I want team members to be happy; conflict bothers me.	• I believe that the director of our team can successfully lead us.	• This project sounds almost too big for a team of four.

Third, analyze the *why behind people's opinions*. This requires discussion, active listening, and clarification of the meaning behind people's words. Remember that people's opinions truly reflect their values. After all, people behave according to their values.

- If you work alone on this case, analyze why the people on the hypothetical team might feel as they do. For example, a team member with a *people orientation* may value team harmony above timely completion of tasks. Compare this to a team member with a *task orientation*: This person may value getting the job done, disregarding the interpersonal cost, because he considers free time so valuable.
- If a small team works on this case, people brainstorm from their own perspectives and then compare all team members' opinions and values. This requires in-depth discussions and probing questions to determine that everyone understands the perspectives of others.

Fourth, agree on a list of team values. The team now consolidates their individual opinions and values from the SWOT analysis chart into a list of team values. Each person must agree to support these team values. The purpose of this step is *not* to reflect every single original opinion and value. This takes discussion and tweaking of the language until everyone is comfortable with the list.

Fifth, transform team values into acceptable team behaviors. Realize that the team's work is not yet finished. A team, after a SWOT analysis and discussion of team values, has established a greater understanding of each other's *opinions and values*. The team has created a common language among themselves—also known as *agreed-upon* team values.

The team, however, has not yet created a list of *acceptable team behaviors*. For example, think about the common team value (also known as a *ground rule*) stated as "respect each other." Teams soon realize, during the heat of the project, that people have different definitions for those words. Therefore, it is now time to rewrite the agreed-upon team values as *acceptable team behaviors*. This step requires people to think behaviorally and specifically.

An easy way to accomplish this is to borrow an item writing technique from survey research. The technique, known as behaviorally anchored rating scales (BARS), helps people envision similar meanings. Please follow the logic of the following example. In essence, you move your team from general, rather disparate information, beliefs, and opinions, to *values and behaviors that everyone agrees to support*.

Let's draw the parallel from survey research by comparing a traditional questionnaire item with a BARS item. Look at the *traditional rating scale item* from a hypothetical questionnaire shown in Box 3-1.

In contrast, look at the BARS item from a hypothetical questionnaire shown in Box 3-2.

Do you see the difference between a *vague* definition of "respect each other" and *behavioral* definitions of respect? For example: Your definition of "a great deal" may be *every time we interact*. In contrast, my definition may be *I'll show you respect when I think your idea makes sense*. Until team members *envision behaviors to define* their values—by *placing behavioral anchors* on those values—they will experience problems because they have not established *shared meanings* for their values. The task of the team, pure and simple, is to select the behavioral anchor that best represents how they want to behave on this project. (It is hoped that most teams would select option 5 among the BARS items!)

BOX 3-1

Traditional Rating Scale Item

Item: Members of our team respect each other . . .

    5 = A great deal
    4 = Often
    3 = Somewhat
    2 = Sometimes
    1 = Never

BOX 3-2

Sample Behaviorally Anchored Rating Scale (BARS)

Item: Members of our team respect each other; this means:

5 = We always actively listen to each other, we paraphrase to establish the true meaning of another person's words, and we explore issues and concepts until we reach a solution that we can all agree to support.

4 = We usually listen to each other, we paraphrase to establish the true meaning of another person's words, and we explore issues and concepts until we reach a solution that we can all agree to support.

3 = We listen to each other when we have time, we double-check what another person said when we are unclear, and we explore issues and concepts until we all agree or until the boss makes the decision.

2 = We try to listen to each other, we guess about what another person meant when we are unclear, and we explore issues and concepts until the most dominant person wins.

1 = We rarely listen to each other, we don't take the time to even guess what another person meant when we are unclear, and we make decisions on issues and concepts without consulting the team.

Move on to the sample solution in Table 3-2 to see a big picture view of the 5-step process. This sample solution reflects the facts provided in the case outlined earlier.

STEP 3: DESIGN THE STRATEGY

The ideas in Table 3-2 comprise a sample solution. Your ideas, and those of your class, will (and should) vary widely. The important feature of this case is to explore what teams gain by moving beyond traditional icebreaker activities to *behaviorally anchored value statements* and *acceptable team behaviors*. Facilitate the SWOT analysis after explaining the project and client information.

TABLE 3-2   Sample Solution for Establishing Values in a New Team (SWOT Analysis Results for a Hypothetical Three-Person Team)

Individual Opinions and Values *(from hypothetical SWOT chart; organized by functional category)*	Agreed-Upon Team Values	Acceptable Team Behaviors
Financial skills: • Strong: Clark, Felicity (also, data analysis) • Weaker: Chris		
Conflict resolution skills: • Strong: Clark • Weaker: Chris, Felicity **Presentation skills:** • Strong: Chris **Writing/grammar skills:** • Strong: Chris • Weaker: Clark **Client perspective skills:** • Strong: Clark	**Value #1** Respect each other.	**Value #1:** Team Behaviors We always actively listen to each other, we paraphrase to establish the true meaning of another person's words, and we explore issues and concepts until we reach a solution that we can all agree to support.
Task completion skills: Strong: Chris, Clark	**Value #2** Capitalize on individual skills without "dumping" on people.	**Value #2:** Team Behaviors We will use individual's strengths to complete tasks efficiently; we will even out the work if and when a person's workload is disproportionately large compared to other team members. We will revisit this issue at least twice a week in team meetings.
Conclusions—Potential Issues (based on team discussions): If the team process is unchecked: Clark and Felicity could run all the numbers, Chris could write and present all the reports, Chris and Felicity could wait for Clark to solve disputes.		

Case 3-2 Interdepartmental Communication Difficulties

(Case purpose: Use bottom-up approach to solve communication flow problems.)

STEP 1: REVIEW THE BIG PICTURE

You manage, for the purposes of this case, a department of 16 people. Your department collaborates on a daily basis with another department comprising eight people. A manager of equivalent tenure and experience runs that department. An ongoing communication issue interferes with the efficient work flow between your respective departments: The people in both departments are not forthcoming with information on a proactive basis. The lack of timely information causes delays and requires individuals to telephone or e-mail people in the other department to request the necessary details.

You and the other manager want to streamline the communications process and you both suggested to your respective departments that people proactively provide others with necessary information. To date, your suggestions have not been followed. You and the other manager are in a planning meeting today; your purpose is to organize an upcoming interdepartmental meeting to identify and resolve the issues causing the slow communications.

Your task is to organize a meeting agenda, identify the people to facilitate the meeting, and specify the group facilitation methods to use during the meeting. You and your colleague are open to co-facilitating the meeting; in addition, you both are comfortable enough in your leadership roles to ask employees from your departments to help facilitate the meeting.

You may need to identify a specific communications flow to serve as the central issue in this case such as the flow of information from and to a project manager with clients, project-based technical and creative experts, and senior management. You will create an agenda to reflect: (1) topical points, (2) facilitators (and their departments), and (3) facilitation methods. You are free to invent departmental and individual names. The author recommends that you consider group facilitation methods such as process flowcharting, brainstorming, or Nominal Group Technique (see Appendix for discussion of these methods).

STEP 2: ANALYZE FACTS AND EMOTIONS (F&Es)

Facts

It is clear that management's top-down recommendation approach has not worked to date. Therefore, it is time that you and your peer manager consider garnering ideas from the bottom up. There may be some detail or specific point in the process flow about which you don't have all the facts; your people may be unwilling to tell you face-to-face why your suggestions won't work.

Emotions

Some managers would worry about opening up a meeting to gather their people's ideas. However, if you truly want to clarify the process flow and identify the problem points, from the points of view of the people performing the work, you must risk hearing their complaints during this meeting.

The trick to facilitating this meeting will be to set aside your managerial feelings that "we might look bad" and focus clearly on process improvement. The meeting agenda should:

- Reflect facilitation by managers as well as experts from the employee ranks.
- Represent an equivalent level of facilitation by both departments, in spite of the fact that one department outnumbers the other.
- Allow for real-time sketches of the current process flow and the desired process flow (to distract people from *us versus them* discussions and focus the entire group on a picture of what successful communications could look like).

The meeting facilitator must rationally explain that the current state of communications isn't working as well as possible and then note that each person in the group has the unique opportunity to create a common picture of the desired state. It is critical, in a meeting like this, to ensure that everyone takes a positive part in discussions and problem solving. The two managers must now allow the *diffusion of responsibility theory* to emerge in this meeting; in other words, employees cannot sit back and wait for the managers or one or two people to step forward with solutions.

The facilitators should, early in the meeting, draw a simple communications flow chart and state that the purpose of the meeting is to improve the process, not to blame people. The facilitators could mark a hypothetical process point or two, using an X symbol, and reiterate that a clear picture of *what we have versus what we want* can help the group focus on what's working and what isn't working. The sketch, drawn near the start of the meeting, helps people talk about the communication flow picture instead of about each other.

STEP 3: DESIGN THE STRATEGY

How you populate Table 3-3 depends on the assumptions you make about the case and the communication flow that you select.

An important point of discussion in this case is to explore why the top-down approach was so vehemently ignored and resisted. Peel back the layers of what might cause such behavior and discuss what other leaders in your group have discovered in their experiences. Do some people resist any ideas just because they seem to be dictated from a source of authority? Do people resist a request because they do not see, and therefore do not value, the need for the change in behavior? Do people understand how to implement the requested change? Is the motivation for change (implied or real) strong enough to bring about the change? Do the leaders demonstrate the desired behaviors in their own daily activities?

TABLE 3-3 Interdepartmental Creative Solutions Meeting

Topic	Facilitator	Facilitation Method	Generate Ideas	Decide Now	Requires Future Action
Introduction	Two managers:	Info sharing			

Case 3-3 Integrating New Technologies

(Case purpose: Roll out new technology to diverse end users.)

STEP 1: REVIEW THE BIG PICTURE

Assume that you are a member of a cross-functional committee comprised of middle level managers in a mid-sized company. A new company-wide system, designed to re-place the legacy systems, will be tested and ready for launch in 3 months. Your commit-tee will decide how to announce the new system. Your committee will also supervise the awareness campaign about the system's new features and benefits as well as the tech-nical training of all managers and employees in all departments.

Your task is to:

- Assume a company name and product/service line in a particular industry.
- Create a communication plan for the announcement, awareness campaign, and technical training. The timeline of your plan should begin prior to the launch 3 months from now and the first round of company-wide awareness and technical training should last no longer than 4 months. Your plan should also include a new-hire awareness and training component. Ensure that senior management, middle management, direct line supervisors, and employees receive information and training. Also include a help-line component.

STEP 2: ANALYZE FACTS AND EMOTIONS (F&Es)

Facts and emotions, as well as training and communication, are inextricably linked in the launch of a new system. Some people greet new systems with enthusiasm while others feel threatened. Some people view training as a waste of time, a free day, or as generic courses taught by people who have never worked in the front line of an organization.

Sometimes the success of a new system lies not in the system itself but in the ability of the trainers and management to convince potential users that the system is valuable enough to learn. (Of course, a few systems are perceived, and rightly so, as too complicated to learn and too cumbersome to use.) Staff trainers cannot successfully communicate with and train a diverse audience of end users without partnering with line managers and employees responsible for specific, functional jobs.

Launching a new system requires strong powers of persuasion: Telling the generic features and benefits of the system is a start; demonstrating, from the points of view of the end users, that the system will make life easier is the true selling point. Often, the staff trainer handles the general information and the line manager covers job-specific procedures. Both often team up to teach troubleshooting steps.

However, even if people are convinced during training that the new system is valuable, post-training troubleshooting procedures may create frustration and verbal help-line rage among nontechnical end users. Common complaints from end users include:

- "My manager is on the committee in charge of training, but did she ask us how we need to use the system day to day? No."
- "This system is so slow that we're finding ways to go around it."
- "I'm spending more time trying to figure out how to use this system than I could have spent completing a week's work using our old system."
- "When I call the help desk, they ask me questions that I can't answer. I'm frustrated by the person who is supposed to help me get unstuck."

Traditionally, troubleshooting procedures treat all end users alike. The questions asked by the help-line expert reflect the point of view of the system: Questions originate from the design and flow of the system. The confused end user doesn't understand this design and flow; if she did, she wouldn't call the help-line in the first place. Companies segment their customers; perhaps system implementation committees should segment their end users, as well. For example, the following help-line expert questions differentiate between a system point of view and an end user point of view—the key is to first recognize the source of emotional frustration experienced by the person and then fact-find and problem-solve (see Table 3-4).

Again, thinking from the end user's point of view, consider some of Diane M. Gayeski's recommendations (p. 115) in *Managing the Communication Function*, for analyzing a training system (see Table 3-5).

All of the considerations noted in Step 2, Analyze Facts and Emotions, should lead the reader to develop a communication plan that considers the range of end users' points of view and that allows for trial and error experiences during the training (somewhat of a discovery learning approach).

STEP 3: DESIGN THE STRATEGY

"Avoid setting yourselves up for failure." Those words of advice come from Mr. Dan Tang, a director for Cost Recovery Corporation. Dan suggests that when technology leaders try to implement a new system "all at once, all groups at the same time," it can be a recipe for failure.

If a new system functions effectively and efficiently, then why would an all-out approach so often result in failure? Mr. Tang suggests that "you're really creating a 'socio-technological' environment, not simply instituting a new technological system." Leaders of a new technological system cannot underestimate people's emotional reactions to a new system.

Mr. Tang recommends that a systems implementation committee first work with a few end user groups and gather opinions through those groups' supervisors. For example, in the case of a new inventory system, "find out what doesn't work for three groups: those needing the inventory items, those managing the inventory, and those purchasing the inventory. Identify how the groups' needs are the same and how they are different." Dan notes that rolling out the new system in phases earns the implementers a benefit: They learn "where you can get advocacy—and how." A few believers in a new system can help train and troubleshoot for the wider audience throughout the organization: Those people become real-time trainers for colleagues experiencing trouble with the system.

TABLE 3-4   Determining Point of View

Questions Derived from a System Point of View	*Questions Derived from End User Point of View*

The following questions can threaten and frustrate the truly novice user:
 	
• What version of XX are you in?
• Have you completed the XX function in the system yet?
• Do you also have the XX application open?
	The following questions segment the callers:
	
	• On a scale of one to three, are you:
	  1. A new user to our company's systems?
	  2. A moderate user of our company's systems?
	  3. An expert user of our company's systems?
	• Please explain the problem you are experiencing.
	• (If the problem is described in the troubleshooting manual provided during training, refer the caller to the appropriate section.) Let's try this . . .

TABLE 3-5   Recommendations—End User's Point of View

Most trainers:	*Most executives and audiences need . . .*
Tell people a single good way to accomplish a task.	Several creative ideas and approaches to tasks and issues.
Tell people how not to make errors.	To experiment, so that they can discover what works best and why.

Refine the bugs in the system and then methodically take the awareness campaign and technical training out to other groups. Mr. Tang recommends that systems implementation committees should want "to minimize the number of calls to help lines in the first place. Categorize people by roles and frequency of usage, and then identify the optimum way to train them."

For example, clerical employees might learn best through a kinetic approach: The trainer or supervisor sits with them during training and explains job aids. Then, those clerical employees can do the same for other people in the organization.

Executives may have different needs all together. Their usage is different: Do executives really *use* the system or do they *need information from* the system? Mr. Tang recommends that the systems implementation committee evaluate the following:

- Has the executive ever used the system in the past?
- If yes, how frequently has the executive used the system?
- Exactly what does the executive need from the system?

For example, an executive may only need to print out a report, get it on to a Web page, and then pull it up, when needed, on a handheld. The bottom line is that different people use a system for different reasons and to varying extents. Dan explains: "Human resources perform administrative functions, trainers conduct awareness and understanding training, and supervisors provide the true application of the policies." Supervisors must perform critical training and troubleshooting functions as a new system is implemented because they help conduct the reality checks about how well the system works.

See Table 3-6 for a sample communication plan. The reader will note the inclusion of help-line experts in the pilot testing and training activities: Too often the help-line experts aren't involved up front and they miss valuable interactions with end users that would assist them later during troubleshooting calls.

TABLE 3-6 Sample Communication Plan: New Technology Implementation

Month Zero (Prelaunch)

Activity	Facilitators	Purpose / Audience
Hold advance meeting	• Senior executive • System committee • Communications expert	Explain final pilot testing and announce launch / Senior management
Hold advance meeting	• System committee • Senior managers • Communications expert	Explain final pilot testing and announce launch and clarify system purpose / Middle management
Hold advance meeting	• System committee • Middle managers	Explain final pilot testing, announce launch, and clarify system purpose / Direct line supervisors
Distribute flier (colorful, heavy paper, suitable for posting on office bulletin boards)	• System committee • Communications expert • Staff trainers	Announce launch, list system purpose and key benefits, and provide help-line numbers / All
Distribute announcement "meeting in a box" (i.e., a set of materials designed to help managers facilitate meetings with their groups)	• System committee • Communications expert • Staff trainers	Announce specifics of launch and group-specific training timeline, reiterate system purpose and key benefits, discuss how new system and your group will interact (e.g., sample meeting agenda, sample materials, sample frequently asked questions) / Managers and direct line supervisors
Send announcement e-mail	• System committee • Communications expert • Staff trainers	Announce launch and general training timeline (by group), list system purpose and key benefits, and provide help-line numbers / All
Reader: What would you add or change?	?	?

Month Zero (Final Pilot Testing, Prelaunch)

Activity	Facilitators	Purpose / Audience
Conduct final round of pilot testing	• System committee • Help-line experts	Identify lingering bugs in system and revise system as needed / Targeted functional work group(s)
Reader: What would you add or change?	?	?

Month 1 (Launch)

Activity	Facilitators	Purpose / Audience
Conduct targeted group technical training pilot	• System committee members • Help-line experts • Staff trainers	Teach system operations and troubleshooting / Targeted managers, direct line supervisors, and selected employees from those groups selected for pilot Start with two or three key groups (e.g., groups that will most frequently use the system, and/or groups that collaborate on critical processes).

(continued)

TABLE 3-6 *(continued)*

Edit targeted group technical training processes and materials, as necessary, for targeted groups	• System committee members • Staff trainers • Managers and direct line supervisors • Help-line experts	Refine training before delivering company-wide / Managers, direct line supervisors, and selected employees from those groups trained in pilot.
Conduct "train-the-trainer" sessions	• System committee members • Staff trainers • Help-line experts	Train targeted managers, direct line supervisors, and selected employees to serve as role models and champions for the new system / Targeted managers, direct line supervisors, and selected employees from pilot test groups
Conduct upper-level technical training	• Communications expert • System committee members • Staff trainers • Managers • Help-line experts	Teach portions of system operations and troubleshooting / Senior management, on an as-needed basis
Reader: what would you add or change?	?	?

Months 2 Through 4 (Technical Training)

Activity	Facilitators	Purpose / Audience
Announce launch success story	• Senior executive • Communications expert • System committee • Staff trainers	Communicate system success and key benefits, include quotable quotes and pictures of people from groups that participated in pilot (perhaps in company newsletter) / All
Conduct managerial-level technical training for company's groups	• System committee • Help line experts • Staff trainers	Teach system operations and troubleshooting / All managers, direct line supervisors, and selected employees from those groups
Edit managerial-level technical training processes and materials, as necessary, for company's groups	• System committee members • Staff trainers • Managers and direct line supervisors • Help line experts	Refine training before delivering to all employees
Conduct all-employee technical training, across company's groups	• System committee members • Staff trainers • Managers and direct line supervisors • Help line experts	Teach system operations and troubleshooting / All employees across all groups
Conduct new-hire awareness and technical training, as part of new-hire orientation	• Staff trainers • Managers and direct line supervisors	Teach system operations and troubleshooting / All new hires across all groups
Refine and revise system as necessary	• TBD	Collect and analyze troubleshooting data; refine and revise system as necessary / TBD
Reader: what would you add or change?	?	?

Case 3-4 Communicating Performance Criteria Changes

(Case purpose: Motivate large employee group to embrace performance changes.)

STEP 1: REVIEW THE BIG PICTURE

In this case, you are an executive with a mid-size U.S.-based company in operation for 12 years. The competition has rapidly passed your organization by; too many of your employees have left for better pay at competitive companies.

In response, for the past 12 months or so, your human resources group worked with division heads and department managers to conduct a salary survey. Employees provided input on their job tasks and performance expectations. Your organization also purchased the services of an outside performance consulting firm, which helped your organization analyze how your company's salary scale compared to those in similar-sized companies within your industry and geographic area. As a result of your analyses, your executive team decided to lead the competition, as opposed to staying even with or following the competition.

It is time to announce the new job descriptions, the revised performance evaluation forms, and the new salary scale. All job categories in your organization are affected.

Your task is to develop a high-level communication plan to announce (for the purposes of this case, you will not prepare the actual communications pieces) the new system. You are free to use any combination of communication vehicles (e.g., e-mail, memo, manager and employee meetings, company newsletters, etc.). You may elect to utilize division heads and managers in division and department meetings. Keep in mind that your audience for this announcement includes virtually everyone in the organization and that different messages must be crafted for different kinds of job titles and people. Select any industry, company, and product and/or service line for the purposes of this case.

STEP 2: ANALYZE FACTS AND EMOTIONS (F&Es)

In essence, division heads and department managers will not want to be blindsided by this announcement. It is critical that the early part of your rollout plan moves top down, so that managers with an emotional need to know will get the right information at the right time.

It is also essential that the plan offers ideas to managers about how to communicate the salary and performance expectation changes to different groups within the organization such as clerical/administrative, technical, and professional. A general announcement might be delivered through a company-wide communication vehicle, followed by specific announcements targeted to particular employee groups. Remember that your executive team decided to lead the competition: This means enhanced salaries, but it also requires improved or different manager and employee performance behaviors. One single-hit announcement will not work; it will take time to announce the changes, explain the implications, and coach people toward desired performance standards.

STEP 3: DESIGN THE STRATEGY

Ms. Kalyn Brantley-McNeal recently joined Hussmann Corporation in St. Louis, Missouri, as manager of human resources and organizational development. She notes that the compensation and human resources strategies are critically linked. Leadership of a company, like the one in this case, that elects to become the company of choice must prepare a complementary message for its people — and with its people.

Ms. Brantley-McNeal states:

> Money is only the initial feature. Environment and relationships, e.g., being challenged by my work, knowing that my ideas are accepted, etc., round out the picture. The money may attract people, but it won't necessarily keep them. Involve people along the way. The changes should not happen to people, the changes should happen with people.

For example, in a previous job, Kalyn "established an Employee Council with volunteer employees (not managers) selected by their peers. The purpose of the council was to provide a sounding board for ideas. The council provided feedback after communications went out and helped to further clarify issues to their peers. An additional benefit of the council was that the group started organizing employee activities."

Ms. Brantley-McNeal stressed that the communication of the new salary ranges, job descriptions, and performance evaluations should not be a one-time event. She suggests that the president or owner meet with the management team to explain and clarify the new system. She suggests including information and materials related to frequently asked questions, how to incorporate the information into leadership training for managers, and how to incorporate the information into career planning and professional development training.

Ms. Brantley-McNeal also suggests covering the new system in new-hire training, and communicating through as many vehicles as possible to ensure that everyone becomes familiar with the details. For example, she used an "HR Corner" on a company Intranet upon which updates were posted on a regular basis. Because different people learn and recall information in different ways, she suggests using print, the Intranet, face-to-face meetings, and other company communication devices.

As a final idea, Kalyn notes that periodic spot checks will help ensure that the new system is implemented correctly; the purpose of the checks is to provide support, encouragement, and coaching. "You can't just tell people once," emphasizes Ms. Brantley-McNeal. Information and new practices must become embedded within the infrastructure of the organization.

Review the high-level communication plan in Table 3-7 and determine what you would change or add. The plan is organized around key messages.

TABLE 3-7   High Level Communication Plan

Key Messages	Support Vehicles (in activity sequence)
Phase One	
1. Salary survey completed: We're behind the competition in salary and performance 2 We want to be the *company of choice* 3. We're taking the following steps to position ourselves out in front . . .	• President meeting with management team • Management meetings with department managers • Department manager meetings with employees • Article in company newsletter • Intranet and memo announcements
Phase Two	
This is what the new system means to our company and our objectives . . .	• Leadership sessions with all managers and direct line supervisors • Breakfast chats with the management team (a series of informal, voluntary half-hour sessions in which employees can ask questions and the management team can reinforce the *company of choice* theme)
Phase Three	
This is what the new system means to our group . . . My job is affected as follows . . . What's working / what's not working	• Department meetings • Department manager meetings with individual employees • New-hire training • Department manager meetings with employees • Management team review and analysis meetings and report to president
Phase Four	
Where are we now: How is this affecting our company and our achievement of objectives?	• President review and analysis sessions with management team • Article in company newsletter • President visits to division-wide meetings

Case 3-5   Changing Course Under Pressure

(Case purpose: Respond to a difficult client situation.)

STEP 1: REVIEW THE BIG PICTURE

Assume that you are a writer working on a consultative basis for a large corporation that manufactures technological equipment (e.g., computers). The marketing manager for that corporation hired you to write the scripts for a video magazine to be sent to salespersons on a regular basis. The video magazine will cover topics such as new product information and sales tips. The theme for the upcoming video magazine, the first edition, is "how to sell to the first time buyer."

The video magazine concept was a long time coming: Executives in your client's corporation could not decide whether to spend the money for the video format, and they disagreed on topics for regular features. You noted some dissention in previous planning meetings with the marketing manager and her staff, and you left the last session rather unclear about what the marketing department collectively wanted. However, your expertise level raised your confidence that you could complete a first script draft that the clients would like. In addition, you and the marketing manager seemed to be on the same wavelength by the end of that last session.

Today, you are in the midst of a video script review meeting with the marketing group. As the session proceeds, some of the marketing specialists nod their heads in agreement with what they see and hear. Your explanations, and the words and script direction before them, seem to meet with their approval. However, the marketing manager suddenly explodes: "What is going on? This is not what we talked about in our last meeting. You're going to have to change it."

Your task is to respond to the marketing manager. What will you say and do?

STEP 2: ANALYZE FACTS AND EMOTIONS (F&Es)

The Facts

The facts are simple:

- The corporate executives, after much discussion, reluctantly decided to try a video format.
- The marketing manager and specialists did not reach true agreement about what they wanted before you left the last planning meeting.
- The marketing manager appeared to like your ideas at the last planning meeting and now she rejects the very concepts upon which you thought you agreed.

The Emotions

The factual indicators should have provided a tip for you: this project had the earmarks, early on, of a potentially difficult project. You should have clearly documented varying ideas on flip charts during the planning meetings, so that everyone could see their points of disagreement. It is too easy to *think* that you've reached agreement, when in fact the group has not: The visual display of ideas can help focus people and help set a common direction.

In addition, the video format is a new concept, so your clients will be somewhat nervous until the video magazine succeeds. Your key client, and her specialists, are fearful of failing in front of their peers and with their ultimate audience for this project, the sales force. You, as a consultant, cannot ignore or minimize the power of such fear.

Last, people often say that they want something, but when they see it they realize that it won't work as well as they originally thought. Clients trying a new concept may not know the right questions to ask; they rely heavily on the consultant. You, as the consultant, should review your advice and behaviors to date. For example:

- Did you ask a series of probing questions to identify where people agreed and where they didn't?
- Did you share nonproprietary samples to display the options available within a video magazine format?
- Did you ask the clients why they ultimately selected the video magazine format? In other words, what do they hope to gain from this format that they wouldn't from a print format?
- Did you spend enough time planning before beginning the actual scripting?

STEP 3: DESIGN THE STRATEGY

Sometimes the answers are so simple that we miss them

This simple question goes to the point of *objectives*: What end result does the client truly desire from the project? What would make the stakeholders *care*?

The more a consultant can trial balloon ideas and concepts, the more likely it is that clients can intelligently and accurately explain their vision of success. Try asking the simple questions—the questions that are too often assumed to have commonly understood answers.

Case 3-6 Using E-mail to Solicit Ideas

(Case purpose: Use e-mail more efficiently to gather ideas from many people.)

STEP 1: REVIEW THE BIG PICTURE

For this case, assume that you are planning a regional sales conference scheduled 9 months from now. You want to gather ideas from your account managers and sales representatives regarding their potential topics of interest. You thought about developing a survey questionnaire but you believe that listing potential topical items would limit the range of ideas too much. You don't have the time to call each person and their schedules make this method of gathering ideas less feasible.

You decide to use the e-mail system to solicit ideas. However, you've received enough poorly worded e-mails to know that your message must be carefully crafted. Your task is to (1) script a brief e-mail message, and (2) succinctly explain the idea solicitation methodology in the e-mail.

STEP 2: ANALYZE FACTS AND EMOTIONS (F&Es)

The bottom line, given the audience, is this: People in sales are busy and they are probably unwilling to read a lengthy e-mail or follow a cumbersome idea-generation process. Your message must first emphasize the benefits of the conference as well as the benefits of offering topic ideas. Second, your instructions for gathering account manager and sales representative ideas must be short and easy to skim. Last, don't forget that some e-mail readers will not read your message, or will delete it, if the subject heading doesn't catch their attention.

STEP 3: DESIGN THE STRATEGY

The writing style that you select depends, obviously, on your organization's culture and expected writing standards. The sample in Table 3-8 outlines the methodology in sample language.

The "$$ Opportunities" would not be limited to cash; the offer could include any acceptable and appropriate item (e.g., vouchers for snacks at the conference site hotel).

TABLE 3-8 Sample E-mail Language

Methodology	Sample E-mail Language
Subject heading that captures attention	Share Ideas, Earn $$ Opportunities
Introduction that delineates benefits	How can you share ideas and earn dollar opportunities? Simple: Tell us what topics you want on this year's sales conference agenda. Why? Because this year's conference can result in more sales for you and better service for our clients *if you tell us* what topics will bring you the most value.
Instructions that are easy to skim	Here's the deal:
The methodology is an adapted Delphi Technique, an established survey process in which the researcher collects information, organizes it for the respondents, and distributes the newly organized list so that respondents have another chance to review and rate specific informational items. (List the items in descending order of frequency: from the most frequently mentioned to those items mentioned by individual respondents.)	First Round: 1. Press *reply* and type in your topic ideas (e.g., new product information, negotiating techniques, what the competition is doing). 2. Receive a check for $xx.xx. If you send us ideas, then we send you a check. Second Round: 3. Look for our next e-mail to you. We'll organize all the ideas that come in. You'll look at that list and rank your favorite ideas. 4. Receive another check for $xx.xx. If you rank that second list of ideas, then we send you another check.
Next steps that have meaning to the sales force	Yes, you'll make money by sending us great ideas. You and the company make money because your ideas help us plan a valuable conference, and the benefits from the conference translate into enhanced sales and customer satisfaction. Everybody wins.

Appendix: Review of Facilitation Tools

Meetings can easily degenerate into meandering conversations or differences of opinion. If you want to facilitate a group of people to think creatively about issues, then try using different group facilitation tools in your meetings.

References are made in this chapter to several group facilitation and idea-generation techniques such as brainstorming, the nominal group technique (NGT), flowcharting, and affinity diagramming. An excellent guidebook to these and many additional tools, is *The Memory Jogger: A Pocket Guide of Tools for Continuous Improvement and Effective Planning* (see this chapter's Bibliography). The following quick overview of the four tools mentioned in this chapter is adapted from *The Memory Jogger*.

BRAINSTORMING

Traditionally, a small group of people focus on a single problem statement (e.g., how to improve productivity by 10 percent within the next quarter?) for up to 1 hour and a half. Five to seven people comprise a manageable group size; however, many people can participate in a brainstorm if they are clustered around small group tables and separate flip charts.

The purpose of a brainstorm is to generate many ideas as opposed to critiquing ideas. A single facilitator may write ideas on a flip chart as people offer comments. Or, with a large group and when time is an issue, the facilitator can post one flip chart sheet per person around the room and everyone can write their ideas simultaneously.

A brainstorm should be fun and, if people feel free to "go into left field" for a time, the quantity and quality of ideas can be astounding. Generate additional ideas by *piggybacking*: A person may combine two ideas

seen on the flip charts and generate a creative hybrid idea.

The results of a brainstorm are the list of ideas; subsequent meetings are usually required to narrow the field of ideas and plan which ideas are most feasible to implement. If it is creative ideas you look for, then invite people from cross-functional areas of your organization (and outside the organization, if allowed): You need people from different disciplines to tackle the problem statement from different angles.

NOMINAL GROUP TECHNIQUE (NGT)

The purpose of an NGT is to help a group reach agreement on an issue so that they may move forward in their planning. An NGT is quite helpful in managing a group that is in dissention or a group that is diverse. The methodology is strict, thus affording everyone an equal voice.

Essentially, the group first generates ideas (see the overview of brainstorming for two potential methods) and lists those ideas on flip chart sheets. Each idea is given a letter: A, B, C, and so on through Z. If ideas still remain, additional items may be numbered AA, BB, CC, through ZZ; and then AAA, BBB, and so on. People explain any ideas that are unclear to others.

Next, similar ideas are combined. The most effective way to combine ideas is to ask people to identify any ideas they view as similar: The ideas are read aloud to the group. The facilitator asks, "Does everyone agree that these items can be combined?" If anyone, even just one individual, responds by saying, "No," then the two items remain separate. For example, if the group agrees that B and FFF are similar enough to be combined, the facilitator draws a thin line through FFF (so that it can still be read), and adds FFF to the letter B. The new and combined item is now designated as B/FFF.

At this point, the group process concludes and people *individually* vote for the five ideas that they like the best. An easy way to complete the individual voting is to give each person five self-adhesive note papers: Each person places a ranking number on each paper as follows:

5 =	4 =	3 =	2 =	1 =

The number five designates the idea *most important* to each person, and one (1) is an important idea, but the *least important* among the five for which a person votes.

One person's five self-adhesive note papers (in an NGT that generated a great many ideas) might read as follows:

5 = BBB	4 = C	3 = RR	2 = Y	1 = B/FFF

After all people complete their individual votes, each person simply places his or her notepapers next to the items on the flip charts for which they voted. It is best to ask people to wait to display their votes until everyone is finished selecting their top five items: You don't want people to follow a highly influential person's voting pattern.

The results of an NGT produce a limited list of ideas upon which a group can then focus their planning attention. An NGT can truly jump start a group of people and launch them into action.

The author used an NGT to facilitate a large group of people attending a session of the St. Louis area's National Conference. The question was, in essence: "What are the watershed events that cause racism in the metro-east area?" A large group of approximately 35 people generated numerous ideas and, as a result, created several action committees (each focused on one of the ideas receiving a high number of votes).

FLOWCHARTING

Flowcharting ties into this casebook's chapter on illustrating concepts (Chapter 5). People can easily run into trouble in their communications because words mean various things to different people and because we may not hear all of what is said—we may hear, but we don't truly listen to the real meaning behind the words. Flowcharting helps a group illustrate the discussion, a concept, a point of disagreement, and thus, flowcharting helps people begin talking about the same thing.

Five standard shapes are used:

- *Oval*—to depict inputs.
- *Box or rectangle*—to identify tasks or activities.
- *Diamond*—to highlight yes/no decision points.
- *Circle*—to depict a break in the flowchart and notify viewers that the chart is continued.
- *Arrow*—to depict directionality between the other shapes.

A flowchart is a consistently good tool to use when a process flow or a communication flow is at risk: The illustration allows people to focus on the picture instead of pointing blame toward others. Also, problem points are easily highlighted on the chart so that subsequent discussions can occur about how to solve specific root causes.

Some people forego the symbols as they initially conceptualize the flowchart, real time, during a meeting. Instead, they arrange self-adhesive note papers on a wall, and re-arrange them as the conversation ensues.

AFFINITY DIAGRAMMING

An affinity diagram serves an essential purpose to a group with many ideas or issues: This tool helps a group organize their thinking—and diversity of opinions—into sensible categories. The most efficient way to conduct an affinity diagram is to start with a problem statement or question.

Then give each person a stack of self-adhesive note papers; ask each person to silently write one idea or solution on each paper. The facilitator will help the group save additional time if she or he asks people to start each idea or solution with a verb. For example, see the following three ideas to solve the problem of "How can we communicate better with our part-time employees?"

1. Provide a written synopsis of key points from department meetings to part-time people.
2. Appoint one full-time person as liaison to the part-time group.
3. Ask part-time people to attend department meetings on a rotating basis (and pay them for it).

Participants then, silently, post their self-adhesive papers on a wall and sort them into meaningful groups. The key here is that everyone posts items and moves items without speaking. When discussions begin, the free flow of ideas stalls. When discussions do start, then the group can decide if the categories make sense. The group can also script headings for each category or grouping.

The results are visual: People can see trends simply by looking at the sheer number of note papers under a given category heading. A person with a divergent opinion can see the extent to which his or her viewpoint is outnumbered.

A FINAL WORD

If your managerial style during meetings is dependent on you asking questions and waiting for people to spontaneously offer answers, honestly evaluate how often which members of your group offer ideas. If your style during meetings finds you doing all the talking, then honestly assess how you can change your meeting facilitation style and identify new group facilitation methods. It may take a while for your people to become accustomed to your new style, but when they do, you should benefit from the quantity and quality of ideas.

Bibliography

Brassard, M., and Ritter, D. (1994). *The Memory Jogger: A Pocket Guide of Tools for Continuous Improvement and Effective Planning*. Salem, NH: GOAL/QPC (1-800-643-4316).

Gayeski, D. (2000). *Managing the Communication Function: Capturing Mindshare for Organiza-* *tional Performance*. San Francisco, CA: International Association of Business Communicators.

Morgan, G. (1997). *Images of Organization*. Thousand Oaks, CA: Sage Publications.

CHAPTER 4

Manager as Meeting Facilitator

Why is a meeting too often a waste of our time?
We treat it as a conversation instead of a project with results.

Introduction

At a minimal level, what defines a project? A project has a reason for being: a *purpose*. A project also concludes with tangible results: *outcomes*. If a manager doesn't focus on these two concepts when planning and implementing projects, that manager probably earns a reputation as a poor project manager. Managers would do well to apply the same purpose and outcomes logic to meetings to avoid earning a reputation for running meetings that are a waste of time.

A manager should spend less time stating *what* the meeting is about (the purpose) and more time *eliciting participation* from people to achieve outcomes (*why* people should care and their resulting *behavioral actions*). This chapter includes cases that require managers to think from the managerial point of view as well as from the meeting attendees' points of view. This shift in focus, similar to the shift required when writing effective business documents, should move meetings along a continuum from conversations to participative events. If you want people to consider new methods, to offer new ideas, and to act on those methods and ideas when they return to their jobs, you most effectively do that by involving them in meetings.

The following cases invite you to explore different ways of planning, implementing, and following up meetings—to transform meetings from dreaded necessities to anticipated events. Creative means of handling meetings are endless; readers will benefit from sharing ideas about these cases.

CASES

Case 4-1   Ask Employees to Think Aloud

(Case purpose: Balance time and technique to coach people more effectively.)

STEP 1: REVIEW THE BIG PICTURE

Assume that you just completed a corporate managerial training class on mentoring and coaching people. You learned a three-step process of how to coach people. You feel that you are now better prepared to teach people new skills and knowledge. As part of your managerial function, you are required to provide on-the-job training to new people as well as tenured people. See the following section for the coaching steps you just learned.

You have a new manager reporting to you; this is the person's first week on the job. The manager has many responsibilities; one task is to help you *(insert a task that you know well here)*.

As a small team (three to five people):

1. Select two people to perform the role-play. One person will coach the new manager on how to *(insert a task that you know well here). Use the "Three Steps to Successful Coaching" (see the following sections).*
2. Note that you should allot the greatest amount of time to "Step 2, Explain the Big Picture and Ask Employee to Outline a Hypothetical Approach."

Three Steps to Successful Coaching

The three steps to successful coaching are outlined here. Refer to Tables 4-1 and 4-2.

1. **Explain the What and Why.** State the *what* (purpose) and *why* (importance and objectives) of your meeting. Use 20 percent of your time for this.
2. **Explain the Big Picture and Ask Employee to Outline a Hypothetical Approach.** Ask the person how and why to approach the issue or task—or how and why it was handled. Actively listen; only interrupt to ask probing or clarifying questions! Use 50 percent of your time for this. (*Note*: The famed violin teacher, Miss Dorothy De-Lay, with former students such as Itzhak Perlman, is known for asking her pupils many questions. Paul Griffiths, in a *New York Times* article, noted that this method causes students to "think about what they are doing and why." The teacher, consequently, helps students "identify other ways of doing things." An excellent manager possesses, after all, skills similar to outstanding coaches and teachers: These individuals know how to get inside the heads of others and motivate them to achieve their greatest potential.)
3. **Coach the Details.** State what is correct about the employee's hypothetical approach. Teach how to improve what wasn't understood or what was missed. Sketch

TABLE 4-1 Three Steps to Successful Coaching		
20% of Time	*50% of Time*	*30% of Time*
Step #1: Explain the What and Why	*Step #2: Explain the Big Picture and Ask Employee to Outline a Hypothetical Approach*	*Step #3: Coach the Details*
• State the purpose of the meeting. • Explain why it is important.	• Explain the basic steps or the basic concept. Don't explain every detail yet. • Ask the employee to outline a hypothetical approach. • Actively listen. • Probe and clarify by asking *how* and *why* questions (to understand how the employee reasons and problem solves). **If you ask the employee questions, you can more easily envision the employee's problem solving skills:** • Remain attentive: focus your eye contact and body direction on the person. Suspend judgment; delay negative emotions such as dismay or anger. • Ask questions and show curiosity: use the *five why* technique (ask *why* until you identify the cause behind the person's thinking). Paraphrase to identify person's values and assumptions (feelings and memories). **A curious manager asks questions and uses practical intuition to achieve creative breakthroughs.** This sentence adapted from R. K. Cooper and A. Sawaf (1997), *Executive EQ: Emotional Intelligence in Leadership and Organizations,* New York: Berkley Publishing Group.	• State what is correct about the employee's hypothetical approach. • Explain what is missing and how to change or improve; sketch a visual to help illustrate the steps or concepts. The picture helps the manager and employee. *See* whether or not their words have similar meanings. (For additional explanation of the visualizing information method, see Chapter 5: "Manager as Concept Illustrator.") • State the benefits of the "correct" approach (i.e., benefits to the employee, the group, the company, the clients).

a visual to illustrate the concept or steps. State the benefits of the approach and how it achieves the intended outcomes. Use 30 percent of your time for this.

STEP 2: ANALYZE FACTS AND EMOTIONS (F&Es)

STEP 3: DESIGN THE STRATEGY

It may help to think through the case from the points of view of a manager and an employee. From the manager's point of view:

• What bottom line tasks does the manager want the employee to complete?
• How would the manager judge "success" on the part of the employee?
• Is there a need to explain common organizational acronyms to the new employee?
• Could the manager provide samples of successful work, or names of others in the organization, that could help pave the way for the employee?

TABLE 4-2 Coaching Tips		

Before the Coaching Session:	*During the Coaching Session:*	*At the Conclusion of Coaching Session:*
Sketch a **visual** to illustrate the issue and a possible solution.	Sketch the visual after conversation is underway. Person must *see* his/her perspectives.	Refer to the visual while agreeing on next steps.
Identify the **behaviors** at issue. A drop file (dated notes on what the person says and does) will help.	State examples of what the person says and does; avoid statements like "your attitude . . ." Assumptions about attitudes can be incorrect and escalate problems.	Restate a few key behaviors to change or improve.
Review the behaviors and identify **trends**.	Listen to one or two answers and say, "I do understand what you are saying." Then state the trends demonstrated by what the person says and does. This avoids the *he said, she said* syndrome about individual situations. Noting the *who*, *what*, *when*, *where*, and *how* (without assuming the *why*) can help prove trends.	Restate how changing/improving a few key behaviors will reduce or eliminate the trends.
Focus on **current** versus **desired/required results,** and the **choices** the person can make.	Clearly state what occurs now and what needs to occur. People respond better to language focused on *results* (not *consequences*).	Note your belief that the person will make the right choices.
List a few **probing techniques** that you can glance at during the session if and when emotions heat up.	Get the person to think out loud: • "I'm not clear on details. Tell me more." • "What do you value about your work?" • "Why did that happen?" (Answer.) "Why do you think that occurred?" (Continue to identify root causes behind symptoms).	Summarize that everyone can maximize results by minimizing negative emotions. Set a follow-up session and, if appropriate, develop a documented action plan (to be signed by relevant parties).

From the employee's point of view:

• What first questions might come to the mind of the employee?
• What processes or procedural points often cause trouble during this task? Might this employee be confused here also?
• Might this employee be afraid to ask questions? (If so, the manager might say, "What else can I tell you about this task?" instead of asking, "Any questions?")

Case 4-2 Give People Control

(Case purpose: Get people more involved by changing how you run meetings.)

STEP 1: REVIEW THE BIG PICTURE

Assume that you understand a crucial point about human behavior: People like control over their daily lives. If people have little control, they can relinquish vital behaviors like caring about outcomes, identifying problems, and creating solutions. If people *perceive* that they have little control, they may simply show up to their jobs without demonstrating any creative caring about how work is accomplished or how others benefit (or suffer) from the quality of their work.

The *number of people* involved in a situation or task can compound the issues inherent in *perceived lack of control*. All too often, the greater the number of people, the less any single person is willing or able to demonstrate individual responsibility. This is the essence of the *diffusion of responsibility theory*, a theory commonly espoused by social scientists. You can see this theory at work in just about any work group, especially during traditionally facilitated department meetings.

A television commercial created for IBM and running during 2000, was a brilliant demonstration of the diffusion of responsibility theory. Several worried people have gathered around a conference table (obviously during off-hours). A woman at the table states that their computer system just crashed and asks people about the various groups involved; for example, the Web group is snowboarding. She finally asks who owns ultimate responsibility for the mess and a colleague whispers, "That would be you." She, of course, looks horrified. Meetings are notorious places for people to feel as though they have no control, and meetings cause some people to wait for someone else to do the thinking: diffusion of responsibility. Managers can, however, write creative agendas to give some control back to people and to cause people to think and participate in meetings.

Assume that you are a manager of a 12-person customer service group (your group responds to customer questions and complaints via inbound telephone lines). Your task in this case is to create an agenda that will turn your next meeting into a lively, interactive experience rather than a scenario in which you speak and everyone else listens or, worse yet, a scenario in which you ask questions and no one in your group comes forward with new ideas.

Develop a meeting agenda for your functional work group's weekly meeting: Your meetings generally run 1.5 hours. You need an agenda to cover the following issues:

- Purpose of meeting
- Group's reaction to president's announcement that company will look into cost-cutting measures this fiscal year
- Group's ideas for where to go for the annual holiday party
- Resignation of marketing director
- Need for better customer service call documentation procedures

STEP 2: ANALYZE FACTS AND EMOTIONS (F&Es)

The first step is to think from your work group's point of view. Imagine that you are sitting in the department meeting: What do you want out of this meeting? Do you want to vote on every single issue? Probably not: You don't want to waste time on administrative trivia. Do you want your voice heard on some issues? Yes. You want to control your work environment and your procedural tasks (see Table 4-3).

STEP 3: DESIGN THE STRATEGY

Review the sample agenda in Table 4-4 to see how this manager illustrates the difference between information ("I'm telling you this") versus interaction ("I need your thinking and participation here").

TABLE 4-3 Planning the Agenda

Topical Points on Agenda	Group's Point of View	Manager's Ideas for Planning the Agenda
Purpose of meeting	Be quick about it; we meet weekly!	Make it short and sweet.
Group's reaction to president's announcement that company will cut costs this fiscal year; departments to create preliminary plans	What does this mean to our group, to me? Do we have any input about what gets cut?	This issue "hits home": people won't like this. Spend meeting time brainstorming how to cut costs in our group.
Group's ideas for where to go for the annual holiday party	The party is fun; the planning is an annual pain. We never agree about where to go; we talk, talk, and talk, every year, about where to go.	The same people will take over. Cost cutting will affect this; discuss after that topic. Try a new tactic: a nominal group technique (NGT) to identify and prioritize ideas.
Resignation of marketing director	Why did the director resign? Does this have any impact on our group?	I'll avoid the rumors; I'll simply state the facts.
Need for better customer service call documentation procedures	What do you mean, need for better documentation procedures? We work hard around here. Are you going to ask us to fill out more paperwork?	Hot issue. Can't finish this in one meeting: ask group to start thinking now, we'll start brainstorming at next meeting.

TABLE 4-4	Sample Agenda

Date of Meeting Agenda
Location
Start and End Times
Key Contact Name and Phone

Person	Time (minutes)	Topic	Info Only	Ideas Needed Now	Make Decision Now	Planning to Come
Manager	2 min.	Welcome; purpose	X			
Manager	4 min.	Marketing director resignation	X			
All	45 min.	Fiscal cost cutting: we control our plan (brainstorm)[a]		X		X
All	30 min.	Annual department holiday party (NGT)[a]		X	X	
All	15 min.	Customer service call documentation: we'll revisit idea at next meeting				X

Date of Next Meeting
Location
Start and End Times
Key Contact Name and Phone

[a]GOAL/QPC offers an excellent pocket guide to group facilitation methods: Brassard, M., and Ritter, D. (1994). *The Memory Jogger: A Pocket Guide of Tools for Continuous Improvement and Effective Planning.* Salem, NH: GOAL/QPC.

Case 4-3   Form Follows Function

(Case purpose: Reinvent how you use space and meeting time for better productivity.)

STEP 1: REVIEW THE BIG PICTURE

Architects know the lesson of *form follows function.* Architects like Frank Lloyd Wright and Mies van der Rohe were known for creating structures devoted to purpose: living spaces, art museums, and office buildings.

People often squeeze into cramped conference rooms and talk through meeting agendas as though doing time in a cell. Unfortunately, the limited facility space (the *form*) often defines the level of interactivity during the meeting (the *function*). The purpose of this case is to help us create new visions of how interactivity can occur, even when limited to small spaces over which we have little control. In essence, the question is how do we function creatively in spite of the form dictated by our preexisting physical work space?

Assume that you run a manufacturing work group representing two direct line supervisors, 24 production line personnel (divided between two shifts), and one administrative assistant. Your group meets (at least twice a month) in a rather confined conference room that doubles as a training room and lunchroom: rows of tables and 20 chairs form a classroom-style setup. An overhead projector, flip chart, and screen complete the setting.

Traditionally, you sit on a table at the front and conduct your meetings looking out at the people. A few people drag in chairs from surrounding offices for the meetings. No one moves around during the meetings (unless they retrieve more coffee) except you, and you walk about when distributing handouts.

Your meetings also traditionally suffer from *diffusion of responsibility* (no one takes real ownership of issues; instead, everyone waits for the management group to do the thinking). You know that your one-way monologue does little to involve everyone, and you plan to run your next meeting differently by using group facilitation techniques.

Your task is to decide how to get people more involved in solving a current production line problem: Supervisors often shut down the line because of malfunctions and resulting quality control issues. How can you involve people before, during, and after the meeting to identify root causes and potential solutions?

STEP 2: ANALYZE FACTS AND EMOTIONS (F&Es)

Clearly, people in this work group have become accustomed to a top-down approach. They see no need to actively participate in meetings, or perhaps they have rarely been rewarded for doing so. The facts (more people need to get involved, but the history of the group does not support this behavior) and the emotions (probably ranging across a wide array of internal thoughts and feelings) conflict.

Internal Evaluation. The manager would benefit from first contemplating his or her own behavior to date, for example:

- What image do I project to my group (e.g., do people believe that I want their help, or that most answers come from me as their leader)?
- Have I asked the right questions in the first place?
- Have I left any time on the agenda, in previous meetings, for open discussion?
- To what extent do I show people that I hear their ideas or concerns (e.g., do I just listen, or do I listen and document their comments on the flip chart)?

Share the Responsibility. Second, the manager needs to pave the way for the new meeting behavior. A manager cannot expect people to walk into a meeting and suddenly leap into action when the modus operandi has been to sit and listen. The smart manager, then, would first engage the two direct line supervisors in open discussions. The opening line for these discussions probably should not be: "I'm going to run our next meeting differently. I'll ask for everyone's ideas, so please tell your people ahead of time to take an active part in the discussion." What is the problem with this tactic? The problem is that diffusion of responsibility is still alive and well: The manager has not given the supervisors a chance to voice any opinions or ideas, and, worse, the manager has presumed that the supervisors don't have any answers. This approach, by definition, would be a real signal that the manager's style inhibits the open exchange of ideas.

Instead, the manager should meet, in an informal and comfortable way (i.e., probably not in the manager's office) with the supervisors and ask them an open-ended question such as: "I'd like to control our meetings less. I believe that you and your employees have valuable ideas and solutions to offer. How might we run the next meeting differently?" First, this tactic uses the "I" approach: People are often more receptive to information when a speaker phrases the request in terms of "I" (a common practice recommended by many therapists). Second, the request is phrased as an open-ended question instead of a directive. The manager, after asking this question, would wait for the supervisors to speak first. (The manager would allow for uncomfortable "dead time," especially if the supervisors weren't accustomed to being asked for their opinions.)

Brainstorm Ideas, Document, and Select a Meeting Approach. The manager should ensure that the supervisors truly believe that they are heard during this meeting. Therefore, all ideas should be documented on a flip chart to prove that open discussion is the new order. If the manager is serious about creating a new culture within the group, one that lasts over the long haul, then the supervisors should take the lead in deciding which approach to use in the upcoming department meeting. The manager would do the supervisors a great favor by empowering them to a greater degree. In the weeks and months to come, the supervisors would gain more respect in the eyes of the employees and would become more motivated to manage the group toward excellence.

Many solutions might work in this situation. See the ideas in Step 3.

STEP 3: DESIGN THE STRATEGY

A range of ideas may work to facilitate the upcoming meeting, given that the supervisors and manager collaborate on the opportunity. Consider the following suggestions, and add ideas from your own experience and thoughts. See the Appendix in Chapter 3, "Review of Facilitation Tools," to help identify which common group facilitation tools might work best.

- Direct line supervisors could hold separate shift meetings with employees to determine "How might we improve working conditions and the quality of our work?" This allows employees to vent first; often, people resist change if they don't believe they have been heard.
- Direct line supervisors would document all ideas and then ask people to select the top three most important ideas: For example, "If we could only have three items on this list, which three would you select?" (Perhaps an NGT would work for this step.)
- Schedule a follow-up meeting to further explore the three most important ideas. Direct line supervisors would compile the lists and the three preferred ideas from the two shifts. Similarities and differences would be discussed. If the lists can be blended, fine. If the shift issues appear markedly different, then two lists would be maintained.
- Supervisors would then ask employees to think about the top three ideas before an upcoming shift meeting (or, perhaps a combined shift meeting). (Allow only a few days between these two meetings so that momentum is not lost.)
- Conduct a second round of shift meetings and explore the reasons behind, and solutions to, the three most important ideas per shift. The supervisor would state that

the ideas most favored by workers would be forwarded to the manager. Again, the supervisor would document all comments and decisions made by the group. (*Consensus* may not be the best method to use when deciding what to take to management. Instead, the supervisors might ask employees to agree that they'll *support selected* ideas, even if all individuals do not agree.) The supervisor would ensure employees that solutions, to the extent possible, will be implemented in the near future. In addition, the supervisors would ask the employees to continue to share their ideas and concerns in upcoming department-wide meetings. The supervisors should probably also provide examples of constructive comments versus debilitating criticism.

- Direct line supervisors would then share, with the manager, the top three answers (from each shift) to the question, "How might we improve working conditions and the quality of our work?" The manager and supervisors would explore the answers, the context surrounding the ideas and opinions, and decide how best to handle the upcoming department-wide meeting.

- The department-wide meeting may best be facilitated by the direct line supervisors. The manager could play a minor role, thus demonstrating the new shift from top-down to collaborative meetings. The manager should, however, clearly explain how the employees' ideas will be addressed: People will not continue to offer ideas if they don't immediately see that their comments have been heard.

Case 4-4 Handling the Unexpected

(Case purpose: Handle being blindsided by a colleague.)

STEP 1: REVIEW THE BIG PICTURE

Assume that you work for a service organization. You work on internal projects and you are known as being a strong meeting facilitator and problem solver. A meeting will occur soon among project team members from your organization, suppliers, and two outside consultants. You are not on this particular team, but the project leader (a respected manager from your organization) called 2 days ago to ask you to attend the upcoming planning meeting. The purpose of the meeting is to streamline the working relationship between your company and the suppliers, with the desired outcomes of containing potential cost increases and reducing the number of delivery problems to customers. The team leader wanted to "get your ideas" at the meeting; you said that you would attend.

The meeting is scheduled for tomorrow morning at 8:00 A.M. You just dashed back into your office (it is now 4:50 P.M.) from a client on-site visit and you retrieved a voice mail from one of the consultants, John. His voice mail (recorded a few minutes ago, at 4:30 P.M.) states: "Hi! I'm just calling about our meeting tomorrow morning. I want to talk to you about how you'll facilitate the last part of the meeting. I have some ideas. I'm leaving the office now, so let's talk in the morning before the meeting. Thanks!"

You are confused; this is the first you've heard that you are facilitating any part of the meeting. You check your e-mail and see that the project leader sent out an agenda for tomorrow's meeting (it was sent earlier that morning). When you open the attached agenda, you see that the project leader is facilitating the first portion of the meeting. Then you see your name listed as facilitating the "Brainstorming and Next Steps" portion of the meeting. Everyone now knows you're one of the facilitators, but no one asked you to take on this function. You call the project team leader and the conversation progresses as follows:

YOU: Hi. I just picked up a voice mail from John. He mentioned that I'm facilitating the last part of our planning meeting but no one told me anything about this. What's going on?

TEAM LEADER: Didn't you get my e-mail?

YOU: Yes, I just saw it. And I see my name listed as a facilitator.

TEAM LEADER: Yes. The meeting won't take more than two hours.

YOU: But the point is that I just learned about this. When you invited me, you didn't ask me to help you facilitate.

TEAM LEADER: Things have been so crazy around here. Client XYZ really put the pressure on us last week; our project deadline was moved up by 7 working days. And, then, you know that we've lost two project members in the last month. What a mess! I'm really sorry, but Client XYZ asked for you specifically. They remembered how you helped to solve that process flow problem last year before their annual stockholder's meeting. They thought you could add great ideas to our current problems.

YOU: So, Client XYZ asked that I help facilitate this meeting? Then, my name must have been suggested in this function a while back, right?

TEAM LEADER: Oh. I just added your name today after I talked to XYZ. I'll take your name off the meeting agenda if you want.

YOU: (You feel that the team leader simply forgot to ask you to help facilitate and is now blaming the issue on other problems.) I'm not asking to be removed from the agenda. I'm actually glad that I missed John's call because it would have blindsided me and made our company seem disorganized! It just seems that . . .

Discuss how you will continue and close this discussion with the team leader.

STEP 2: ANALYZE FACTS AND EMOTIONS (F&Es)

This case may seem like a simple "no brainer." However, the political ramifications of *how* you say what you say could have far-reaching effects, depending on the power bases held by you and the team leader (and how the team leader handles what is said about you). Ask the questions in Table 4-5 to help you determine what to say to the team leader—and how to say it.

STEP 3: DESIGN THE STRATEGY

You are clearly a valued member of your organization, and as such, people sometimes request that you take on additional tasks. If you do not participate, in terms of risk management, your reputation could be at stake: People would see your name on the

TABLE 4-5 Deciding What to Say	
Factual Questions	*Emotional Questions*
• Is my participation crucial to the outcome of this planning meeting?	• Why does the team leader seem to avoid taking responsibility for the mix up? How can I reassure the team leader that mistakes are acceptable if and when we own the problem and the solution?
• What's in it for me?	
• If I don't participate, what might the repercussions be to my reputation?	
• If I participate, what are the facts I need to know now?	• Should I allow my annoyance to drive my decision to participate or not participate?
• If I participate, do I meet with the consultant alone tomorrow morning, or do I ask that the team leader meet with both of us?	• In my conversation, how do I balance (through what I say, how I say it, and through my tone of voice) the following facts and emotions:
• How do I communicate to the team leader that this cannot happen again?	❑ Do I push the team leader to admit the mistake?
• If I participate, do I select a group facilitation technique now or do I wait to see how the meeting progresses?	❑ Do I just ask for the facts now and express my annoyance later?
	❑ Do I confront the team leader about the peripheral excuses and ask to return to the problem at hand?

agenda but learn that you "could not attend." This may call into question your dedication, depending on *how* the team leader delivers this news to the meeting attendees (and to others outside of the meeting). It is not worth your while to make an enemy of the team leader. It is, however, probably worth your while to function as a value-added corporate citizen and also to coach the team leader on acceptable behavior (without creating an enemy).

Your conversation may continue, and conclude, in a fashion similar to that outlined in Table 4-6.

TABLE 4-6 Finishing the Conversation

What you might say:	*Why you say it this way:*
"It just seems that the primary issue is how I can best prepare to support you in the meeting tomorrow. The secondary issue is the oversight in informing me of my role. What's important now, especially given the project and personnel issues you're experiencing, is to run an effective meeting tomorrow morning. If you tell me what I need to know about the current issues and ideas, then we can organize the meeting to look good and achieve what you need."	You perceive your participation as crucial because of the team leader's position of power and because of the potential risk to your reputation. You are not cooperating out of fear; you decide to cooperate because this is not a war worth fighting. So focus on facts and minimize emotions.
	The team leader is not taking responsibility (for reasons you can only assume) and now is not the time to assume a confrontational posture that may only cause the team leader to become defensive.
	The framing of the if/then statement places responsibility on the team leader and promises positive outcomes stated in the point of view of the team leader.
After hearing the team leader's perspective: "Great—now I have a clearer picture of what we need to do. I'll select a facilitation technique during the meeting rather than arbitrarily selecting one now. That way, we'll first see how willing people are to participate in a constructive solution. The flow of the meeting will tell me which technique might yield us the best results."	For now, you hold on pushing the team leader to admit the mistake; you won't buy any value from pushing this point now.
	You get to the bottom line facts and position yourself on the same side of the problem with the team leader.
	You highlight the benefits of running the latter portion of the meeting your way (i.e., select a technique later). This way, if the meeting progresses in an unforeseen way, you aren't stuck with a facilitation technique that won't fit the context.
"Let's meet with John fifteen minutes before the meeting tomorrow to hear his ideas and outline our plan."	The three of you must meet: You cannot be left out of the loop again, and, you cannot leave the team leader out of the critical conversation with the consultant.
	Your plan is flexible enough, by the way, to require little modification no matter what ideas John has.
After the meeting, when everyone feels good about an effective meeting run efficiently: "Balls get dropped when we get busy. I'm glad that we took the time to plan our strategy before we stood before your team, the suppliers, and the consultants. If you need my help again, let's quickly touch base ahead of time."	You never confronted the team leader head on. You took a circuitous route, but the team leader still got the message. You're willing to help him/her look good and solve problems, and you require advance planning to do so.
	If the meeting went well, the team leader (if a reasonable person) will give you credit.

Case 4-5 What Kind of Meeting Is This, Anyway?

(Case purpose: Help your management team run better meetings.)

STEP 1: REVIEW THE BIG PICTURE

In this case, you need to educate your technical managers about how to run meetings. You direct a large division, and the employee satisfaction survey results once again portray a sad story about department meetings. The most common complaints among people read something like this: "What is the purpose of our meetings, anyway? We never seem to get anything accomplished. Why do we even need to meet?" Or, "Are we supposed to just talk about this stuff or make some kind of decision? Our manager asks for an answer to a problem and we all sit there. So who is supposed to have the answers around here, anyway?"

You believe that employees could, and would, more actively participate in meetings if your managers knew how to run them more effectively. Your task is to develop an agenda that you can use when educating your 20 managers about running effective meetings (without *telling* them what to do).

STEP 2: ANALYZE FACTS AND EMOTIONS (F&Es)

First, Consider the Emotions. Many managers believe that they do run effective meetings, so the director in this case would be advised not to *tell* managers how to facilitate meetings. The director might get more mileage out of an *embedded approach*. In other words, the director could start modeling the desired meeting facilitation behaviors in her own division meetings.

You must know *what* you want to teach before you can decide *how* to communicate it. However, the *audience* comprises valuable and highly skilled managers, and if the director disregards the egos of such an audience, then a typical "I'll tell you what to do" approach (i.e., the easiest approach) might be selected by that director. This, alas, would be a mistake.

Second, Outline the Facts. Taggart E. Smith, in the book *Meeting Management*, lists four kinds of meetings (pp. 41–42):

1. Information-giving meetings
2. Information-exchange meetings
3. Problem-solving meetings
4. Decision-making meetings

The *information-giving meeting*, according to Smith, is best used when a manager wants to talk about programs or policies, when a team wants to sell to a client, when process or procedures training is needed, or when team motivation needs enhancing.

The *information-exchange meeting* is a good strategy when information is complicated or when people may disagree, when the meeting audience would be highly affected by the information, or when personal interaction is required to maintain or establish connections among people.

The *problem-solving meeting* is a good choice when a manager needs a quick solution, when employees identify service or product problems, when conflicts are in evidence, or when people must be persuaded to think or behave differently.

The *decision-making meeting* is best used when problems have been discussed but not yet finalized or when people must make a decision or an evaluation of something.

Review the Appendix to Chapter 3: "Review of Facilitation Tools."

STEP 3: DESIGN THE STRATEGY

The director in this case might elect to facilitate a series of regular division meetings in which he or she applies and demonstrates the four kinds of meetings. For example, review the division meeting agendas in Tables 4-7 through 4-9 to see how this director applied Taggart Smith's concepts.

TABLE 4-7   Agenda 1

Division Meeting: Friday, November 10
Central Conference Room
9:00 A.M.–10:30 A.M.
E. James, Director (ext. 3737)

Responsible	Time (min)	Topic	Info-Giving Meeting	Info-Exchange Meeting	Problem-Solving Meeting	Decision-Making Meeting
Director	15	New division business / status reports		X	X	
Director	30	Employee satisfaction survey results	X			
Managers	35	Managers' points of view on survey results: open discussion of problems and root causes (documented by director on flip chart)		X		
Director	15	Request: think about potential solutions to employee satisfaction issues	X			

Next Meeting: Friday, December 8
Central Conference Room
9:00 A.M.–10:30 A.M.
E. James, Director (ext. 3737)

TABLE 4-8   Agenda 2

Division Meeting: Friday, December 8
Central Conference Room
9:00 A.M.–10:30 A.M.
E. James, Director (ext. 3737)

Responsible	Time (min)	Topic	Info-Giving Meeting	Info-Exchange Meeting	Problem-Solving Meeting	Decision-Making Meeting
Director	15	New division business / status reports	X	X		
Managers	30	Round robin reporting of ideas: potential solutions to employee satisfaction issues (documented by director on flip chart)		X		
All	45	Reading and clarification of each idea, followed by voting of three most important ideas (e.g., using an NGT)			X	
Director	02	Request: think about which important ideas to implement first	X			

Next Meeting: Friday, January 12
Central Conference Room
9:00 A.M.–10:30 A.M.
E. James, Director (ext. 3737)

TABLE 1-9   Agenda 3

Division Meeting: Friday, January 12
Central Conference Room
9:00 A.M.–10:30 A.M.
E. James, Director (ext. 3737)

Responsible	Time (min)	Topic	Info-Giving Meeting	Info-Exchange Meeting	Problem-Solving Meeting	Decision-Making Meeting
Director	15	New division business / status reports	X	X		
Small teams of managers	45	Explore which important ideas (generated from previous meeting) to implement first, and why			X	X
Leader of each small team	30	Report results of small manager team discussions		X		
Director	02	Request: I'll e-mail typed results of team discussions; be ready to decide on final implementation ideas in our next meeting	X			

Next Meeting: February 9
Central Conference Room
9:00 A.M.–10:30 A.M.
E. James, Director (ext. 3737)

Case 4-6 Regaining Control of a Meeting

(Case purpose: Regain control of a meeting when your agenda is ignored.)

STEP 1: REVIEW THE BIG PICTURE

In this case, you are running a meeting comprised of your managerial peers. You are 30 minutes into the 2-hour meeting and you begin to experience problems. Two managers want to discuss another topic; their reason is that until the other topic is settled, the group cannot reach consensus on this meeting's topic. In fact, the two managers blatantly ignore you and now try to run their own meeting, to the exclusion of your agenda.

There are 10 managers in the meeting: They represent the functional groups of your company. Two managers are wrestling you for control of the meeting while the other eight participants are increasingly frustrated. You are not the direct line supervisor of any person in the room; the company president, at the last meeting, asked you to facilitate this meeting in her absence today.

Your task is to create specific details (e.g., today's topic and the off-point topic favored by the two managers), then, hypothetically go back in time. If you could plan the perfect meeting, how would you organize this meeting to keep it from going astray? Points you might consider include:

- Agenda (including location, timing during the day, which day of week, number and kind of facilitators)
- Meeting ground rules
- Room arrangement
- Roles and responsibilities of attendees (just attending is not enough)
- Devices to use in the event of disruptions (e.g., list concerns on flip chart "parking lot")
- Personal strategies to use in the event of conflict (e.g., avoid verbal altercations)

This case works well as a simulation. A small group of five people could portray enough roles and personalities to make the simulation work. The point is to enact a meeting and then debrief to identify:

- Planning strategies that could have been handled differently.
- The problem points in the meeting.
- How the facilitator could have handled the problems differently.
- Personal experiences and suggestions for handling difficult meetings.

STEP 2: ANALYZE FACTS AND EMOTIONS (F&Es)

The facts are seemingly simple: The company president asked a manager to facilitate the managers' meeting in the president's absence. Additional case facts are based on the assumptions and specific information made by the readers.

The emotions in a situation like this can be quite complex. Is the manager in charge of this meeting perceived as the company president's "favorite child?" If yes, then the behavior demonstrated by the two managers could be founded on pure jealousy and mean-spiritedness. In that case, the manager facilitator should have lobbied for support from other managers before this meeting ever began. In addition, the company president and manager should have talked, so that the president could have then clarified behavioral expectations to the entire management team prior to the meeting. This manager needs "air cover": Without it, the meeting agenda and the manager's credibility may quickly erode.

Are the two dissenting managers known for their off-task meeting behavior? If yes, then the company president and manager facilitator might have considered asking these two to take on critical roles (e.g.: scribe at the flip chart, topical point timekeeper, etc.).

Is the topic in question being handled via informal, open discussion? If yes, then a stronger facilitation method might be in order (see Appendix to Chapter 3: "Review of Facilitation Tools").

Did the president leave specific orders for results from this meeting (e.g., action plan, list of critical barriers, people designated as project leaders)? If yes, did the president communicate this expectation to the entire management team, or just to the manager facilitator? The president must take on vital responsibility here: he or she cannot expect everyone to listen and cooperate just because an interim meeting facilitator says, "the president wants it this way." The president must pave the way for the manager facilitator by clearly communicating expectations, next steps, and desired outcomes to all managers before the meeting occurs.

STEP 3: DESIGN THE STRATEGY

Use the checklist in Table 4-10 to help you design the perfect meeting. Add to or edit the list as necessary, given the case details that you select.

TABLE 4-10   Checklist for Designing the Perfect Meeting

Planning the Perfect Meeting	
Points to Consider	*Checklist*
Agenda	❑ Select best location: adequate room size, flip charts, markers, etc. ❑ Select best timing during the day: least likely to interfere with managerial duties or crises ❑ Select best day of week: least busy given overall work flow ❑ Include appropriate number and kinds of facilitators: adequate position power of meeting facilitator or, in case of delegated responsibility, supervisor clearly communicates delegated authority prior to meeting ❑ Distribute agenda prior to meeting (see sample agendas in this chapter) ❑ Display extra copies of agenda at entry to room ❑ Clearly document and review next steps and persons responsible at end of meeting
Ground rules	❑ Create ground rules that all group members will agree to support ❑ Clearly communicate ground rules within group and at start of meetings ❑ Post the ground rules in visible spot during meetings, especially if conflict is expected ❑ Remind participants of ground rules as needed
Room arrangement	❑ Turn off all phones unless a critical call is expected ❑ Avoid classroom style seating unless meeting is informational only ❑ Arrange tables and chairs prior to meeting to match purpose of meeting (e.g., conference table or U-shaped for discussions, small table groupings for small team work) ❑ Position adequate supply of visual aids (e.g., flip charts, markers, blank overhead cells, etc.) to facilitate real time documentation of ideas and the illustration and editing of those ideas
Roles and responsibilities	❑ Appoint a lead facilitator ❑ Appoint co-facilitators as needed for topical points on the agenda (to enhance participation) ❑ Appoint a scribe to document ideas and comments ❑ Ensure that everyone is aware of roles and responsibilities for next steps (best to document this on flip chart and ask individuals to clarify their understanding of tasks before ending the meeting)
Devices for avoiding or minimizing disruption	❑ Prior to the meeting, match a group facilitation method to the topical points on the agenda (rather than just talking to the group on every point) ❑ At start of meeting, review agenda and ground rules; also state meeting purpose and desired outcomes ❑ Ensure that the facilitator remains active: maintain group energy by physically moving about the room ❑ Move toward disruptive people (the facilitator's presence may stop the off-task behavior)

TABLE 4-10   *(continued)*

Planning the Perfect Meeting

Points to Consider	Checklist
Personal strategies for handling conflict	❏ Enforce the agenda and ground rules ❏ Reiterate meeting purpose and desired outcomes ❏ Clearly defer off-task issues to a parking lot on a flip chart, promising the dissenters that they'll be heard in the near future ❏ Remain neutral: do not take sides or discount a person's opinion ❏ Remain calm under pressure: a facilitator's credibility depends on it ❏ Request that a point be held for a moment, and return to the task at hand (to help deflect any hostility or anger) ❏ Maintain eye contact with entire group; don't get locked into a one-on-one with a hostile attendee ❏ Call a brief break, if necessary
Other	

Bibliography

Brassard, M., and Ritter, D. (1994). *The Memory Jogger: A Pocket Guide of Tools for Continuous Improvement and Effective Planning.* Salem, NH: GOAL/QPC (1-800-643-4316).

Cooper, R. K., and Sawaf, A. (1997). *Executive EQ: Emotional Intelligence in Leadership and Organizations.* New York: The Berkley Publishing Group.

Griffiths, P. (2000, September 3). How a teacher can influence a whole life, *New York Times*, p. AR27.

Smith, T. E. (2001). *Meeting Management.* Upper Saddle River, NJ: Prentice Hall.

CHAPTER **5**

Manager as Concept Illustrator

The Fourth Wall Metaphor
Cases:
      5-1: Example
      5-2: Mini Cases
Bibliography

There is an invisible wall between us.
A picture that tells a story creates a bridge over that wall.

The Fourth Wall Metaphor

A concept well known in theater may be applied to managerial communications. On a traditional theater set, two sidewalls and a back wall exist. Audience and actors are aware of these walls and can clearly see them. However, an unseen wall exists in theater productions; this invisible space along the front edge of the stage is called the *fourth wall*. It is, simply stated, an invisible wall between audience and actors.

Actors must invent, in their minds, a fourth wall to separate them from the audience. Actors must *see* an open window and billowing curtains, *see* a cat curled in a corner love seat, *see* pictures on that fourth wall. For it is this fourth wall, invented in the actors' minds, that precipitates unwanted eye contact between audience and actor.

Actors train to effectively build a fourth wall. The rest of us, daily, protect ourselves behind an unseen wall or attempt to bridge that unseen barrier when we reach out to others. We spend lifetimes learning tools and techniques to manage an invisible wall.

THINK VISUALLY TO BRIDGE THE WALL

In this author's work with MBA students (full-time, professional, and executive), we work through a module entitled *Visualizing Information*. The purpose of the Visualizing Information module is to hear words and translate them into pictures. A business school does not train people to become architects, so why incorporate such a module?

Let me answer that question with two questions.

1. How many meetings have you experienced in which people talked and talked, disagreed, came to consensus on a few points, and then talked some more—resulting in a tremendous waste of your time?
2. How many times have you participated in meetings in which much of what was discussed in earlier meetings was rehashed again—and with few new outcomes?

The bottom line is this: few meetings are short enough, few people mean the same thing even when they use similar words, and few people truly leave the majority of meetings with a common view of what will happen next. One way to shorten meeting time, bridge the gap between word meanings, and allow people to leave with a common version of next steps is to *visualize the information*.

This is not a simple skill; it takes time to learn to think visually. It requires practice, it demands discussion about what the same picture means to different people, and it means watching how others formulate visuals. Then, and only then, can most of us feel comfortable portraying concepts, issues, plans, and solutions in a visual manner. (Architects and engineers, by definition of their training, are exceptions.)

This chapter is free flowing when compared to the other chapters. The best way to work through this chapter is with other people; this author suggests conducting loosely structured brainstorming sessions comprised of people from varying disciplines. A small group of people, each representing a different area (e.g., marketing, operations, engineering, manufacturing, or finance), will produce widely varying freehand illustrations. Only by comparing different styles will we learn to comfortably sketch concepts and words in real time during our meetings. The sample illustrations in this chapter serve as thought starters.

CASES

Case 5-1 Example

STEP 1: REVIEW THE BIG PICTURE

For the purposes of this case example, assume that you are a faculty member at a business school. You asked a respected business owner to discuss an issue from his organization with your MBA class. Use the following case as an example to work through before reading the mini cases in this chapter. This author's (i.e., the faculty member's) actual conversation with the business owner is paraphrased here as the case example.

A business acquaintance of mine, Mr. Doug Harbison, agreed to talk about his organization with one of my MBA classes. Doug owns EVER Corporation, with administrative offices located in St. Louis and a plant in Arkansas. EVER manufactures collapsible aluminum tubes (the kind used in petroleum jelly products and ophthalmology products).

Doug was in my university office to outline what he would discuss with my class; he was scheduled to visit my class twice. Doug would first explain his business and its issues and answer students' questions. He would return in a few weeks to hear their presentations about how to solve his business issues. At our initial meeting, Doug gave the following overview:

I bought that company when it was in desperate need of a turnaround. The performance was on a flat line. After I bought it, the bottom fell out. Everything seemed to go wrong. I'd gone out and sold a bunch of new business, but our production line couldn't keep up and the quality problems soared.

We worked for months. Finally, performance started to creep back up. It went as far as the original flat line and stalled out. Now, over the last few months, we're seeing some improvements. Performance is creeping up and we're stabilizing.

Things have recently started to pop. We really function as a team now. I hired some great people away from the competition. But now I have a new problem. We foresee that in the new quarter our improvements will really show value.

It will be like an air-filled bottle held under water. You know what happens to that bottle when you let it go? It just skyrockets! Our sales are going to soar and then I'm afraid our production line and quality issues might return—only it will be more critical than before because we'll have to produce at such a fast rate.

STEP 2: ANALYZE THE FACTS AND EMOTIONS (F&Es)

As Doug talked, I noted on paper the chronology of events, I watched his body language, and I listened to the inflections in his voice. Indeed, the *facts* (the company could experience more trouble) and his *emotions* (he was worried) matched up—and for good reason. I could *feel* this man's passion about his investment and about the business itself. I clearly *saw* and *heard* that Doug cared about the people employed at that plant.

The Facts and Emotions. Doug knew that if he didn't successfully complete the turn-around, many people could be in jeopardy. The plant's location in a small Arkansas town would make it difficult for people to find new employment (the facts). This highly successful man was smart enough to look ahead to a critical point in time in the near future; *this* was the critical point of Doug's *emotions*. He was concerned about that future point at which production could soar: His production line must ensure quality delivery on more orders.

The Bridge Between Us. I knew that if I simply took notes, assured Doug that our students would have great ideas, and then sent him on his way, I could miss a critical point of connection with him. But, I was worried myself. He did seem to perch on the precipice of potential success or potential failure; there would be little leeway for previously acceptable production and quality levels.

Little did I know that a simple picture, sketched in pen on a notepad, held the *communication turning point* for our meeting. As Doug talked, I mingled my longhand notes with a sketch. Table 5-1 illustrates how this sketch (i.e., the *bridge*) evolved and how a simple sketch successfully *met the force* of his emotion.

When Doug saw that my sketch mirrored his company facts and his emotions (especially the last upward "air in a bottle" line), he jumped forward in his chair and said, "That's it! That's it! If we can turn this thing around—and I believe we can—then we're still in trouble if we can't meet the new production needs!"

TABLE 5-1   Evolution of the Picture

Doug's Words	*How the Picture Evolved*
"The performance was on a **flat line**."	I drew a simple horizontal line on my page.
"After I bought it, the **bottom fell out**."	I etched the line on a downward nosedive.
"Finally, **performance started to creep back up**. It **went as far as the original flat line and stalled out**."	I brought the line back up, slowly and in halting steps, and finally stopped it at the original point of the nosedive. Then I continued a simple horizontal line to the right.
"Performance **is creeping up and we're stabilizing**."	I now sketched the line in a gentle upward slope.
"It will be like an air-filled bottle held under water. You know what happens to that bottle **when you let it go! It just skyrockets! Our sales are going to soar** and then I'm afraid our production line and quality issues will simply return—only it will be more critical than before because we'll have to produce at such a fast rate."	His bottle metaphor creatd the bridge between us—I let the line fly straight up to the top of the page.

STEP 3: DESIGN THE STRATEGY

Doug sat back and the energy in the room immediately shifted. He seemed *convinced* that I understood his dilemma. He *believed* that I understood what he was trying to say. What had convinced him? What had caused Doug to suspend his disbelief that anyone else could understand his situation?

His metaphor *(the bottle)*, in conjunction with a simple sketch *(a trend line),* became the *bridge* for our communication. I visualized what he experienced; he saw that I understood his story. That was the point at which a bridge was built. I recounted that conversation to my class (without showing them my visual). I asked the students to draw their own sketches of the conversation. Many of them found the concept of drawing a conversation new, yet a couple students immediately grasped the concept. I asked those students to copy their drawings on the chalkboard. As they drew, others watched and began to conceptualize that you can *visualize a client's words and emotions.* This exercise allowed them to *see* Doug's passion for the business, his potential production dilemma, and his need for quick answers. I wanted them to interact with Doug in a dynamic way (not like a typical class of 20 students passively listening to a guest speaker), and it required enthusiasm and dynamic, conceptual thinking.

When Doug met the students, they operated in vibrant teams: They structured their questions and participated in a conference call with his vice president of sales and the plant manager. Doug's energy and commitment challenged them to creative thinking. Everyone worked forward from a mutually agreed upon, one-sentence problem statement: *How can we see results from interventions now, before EVER Corporation's sales jump (to avoid resurfacing previous problems)?*

A single picture became the bridge, the story, between client and student consultants; the picture helped us formulate a clear problem statement and the story jumpstarted the students' creation of solution ideas.

I became a believer in the power of a *picture as bridge and metaphor.* Apparently I'm not the first to arrive at this conclusion. Ms. Karen Berg, chief executive of Commcore Communication Strategies in White Plains, was quoted by Eric Quiñones in the *New York Times*: "Anything that engages the mind's eye is more memorable than just getting up and spouting off data. They will remember the visual images."

Indeed they will.

✳ Case 5-2   Mini Cases

Assume that each mini case in Table 5-2 represents a conversation between you and a client (either internal or external). Your task, for each mini case, is to translate the client's words into a *visual that creates a bridge between the two of you.* A creative way

TABLE 5-2 Mini Cases

Case	Step 1: Review the Big Picture
2a	Our process flow is a mess. We're stuck in the same loop—we're just repeating the same mistakes over and over again.
2b	We sit in a precarious sales position because 85 percent of our sales come from 15 percent of our customers. We need a better balance—perhaps 70/30.
2c	On the surface, sales look successful. However, in reality, it's like they're marching down a field in single file. You see, one lead salesperson is always first—she's been the sales leader for the past 3 years. All the rest of the salespeople follow right behind this gal! I want to jump start more of them. I want several of them to compete for that top spot every quarter!
2d	There is too much overlap among those three departments! I'm tired of trying to settle their interdepartmental wars. Can't we just merge them? I'm serious about this. There is a lot of overlap among their skill sets and projects, you know.
2e	We're at cross-purposes here. You two get on the same page on this project or I'll make a staffing change!
2f	Our processes are too confused. The complexity is overwhelming. No less than nine people across four different departments touch a single purchase order! We need to simplify things around here!
2g	We are so internally focused lately! I hear our people complain constantly that they can't complete client work because of our internal process improvement initiatives. Why aren't we thinking about our customers anymore?
2h	We spend too much time talking and not enough time listening. Are we focused on any one goal here?
2i	I know things look bleak now, but the investment in cleaning up our production line efficiency is significant. We've made great progress, actually. These changes should begin to pay off. The bottom line is that the benefits to our P&L Statement should really kick in within the next quarter!
2j	We've been moving so fast! We're missing a lot of important information and details. Too many mistakes have been made on projects for our three best clients. We need to find a way to slow down and be more certain of our service accuracy and overall quality.
2k	Look, we have a problem here. As a sales manager, she's supposed to spend at least 30 percent of her time in the field coaching! But I know for a fact that she only goes out about 10 percent of the time. Her performance review is coming up and, just so you know, she and I have had this conversation before! How do I make it clear that she has to get out of that office more often?

to approach this is to work as a team on each conversation; then compare the drawings among the teams to see varying thinking styles. Identify how some styles are literal and others are more representational.

The sample solutions (adapted from hand drawn sketches) are illustrated in Table 5-3. The point is to learn to sketch visuals in real time during meetings; you can do this without becoming a computer graphics expert.

Ms. Betsy Ley, a St. Louis-based graphics wizard and assistant to an extremely fortunate company president, created the illustrations.

Table 5-4 presents some suggestions for visualizing information.

TABLE 5-3   Sample Solutions

Step #2 *Analyze the Facts and Emotions (F&Es)*	*Step #3* *Design the Strategy*

Case 2a

The critical feature of this visual is that it must portray a *barrier* to movement. The illustration must capture *the feeling of frustration* caused by repetitive process problems.

Case 2b

The key element of this graphic is *balance*—or lack of it. People need to sense the pressure they're under because too few customers control too much of the company's revenues.

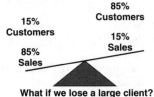

Case 2c

There are two critical elements to this illustration: first, the *appearance of success* that shows above the water line and second, the *motivational root causes* underlying the poorly distributed sales among the majority of salespeople.

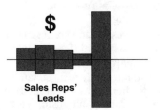

Case 2d

The key in this situation is to focus on the *facts* and minimize the emotions. A simple Venn diagram can hold words outlining critical functions and tasks; then, people can see whether or not the three departments truly overlap in critical functions.

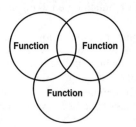

Case 2e

The simple approach is to draw two arrows representing two people at odds with each other. However, a better illustration visualizes the *impact of their behavior* on the health of the project.

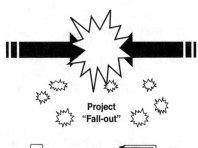

Case 2f

This requires *before and after* process flows. Pure and simple, the picture will tell the story.

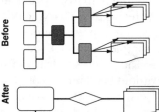

TABLE 5-3 *(continued)*

Step #2 ***Analyze the Facts and Emotions (F&Es)***	*Step #3* ***Design the Strategy***

Case 2g

This picture must carefully reflect the need for process improvement *and* customer satisfaction. The visual must not enhance one to the exclusion of the other. *Focus* on a common end goal is the key here.

Internal Process Improvement

Meeting Customer Needs

Case 2h

This statement is easy to visualize; it is not so easy to draw. The temptation is to draw a gaping mouth and a tiny ear; that only misses the true point of *focus on a common end goal*.

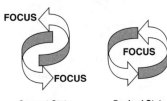

Current State   Desired State

Case 2i

Two variables are at play here: production line *efficiency* and bottom line *results*. This visual must clearly delineate the correlation between the two.

P & L Statement

Case 2j

Sometimes the best way to illustrate *numerous, recurring problems* is through a *simple drawing*. Stick figures, that anyone could sketch *real time* on a flip chart during a meeting, can provide a powerful metaphor for continuous improvement discussions. A side benefit is that the metaphor of "dropping the baton" minimizes the finger pointing at any one person or department and instead emphasizes the responsibility of everyone in generating a long-term solution.

Case 2k

The best way to illustrate this issue is by correlating *percentage of time* to *sales results*. The intended recipient of this "lecture" is a sales manager: a person highly motivated by revenues and results.

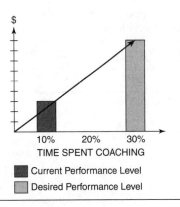

Source: Used with permission of Betsy Ley.

TABLE 5-4 Quick Study to Visualizing Information[a]		
To Illustrate/Compare:	*Use . . .*	*Pros/Cons*
Component: (percentage of a total) Show size of each part as a percentage of total. Conversation Tip-offs (see note): Share, percentage of total, accounted for X percent. *Note:* Conversation Tip-offs refer to the words used or the requests for information you hear during conversations.	**Pie chart** (at specific time) **Two pies, columns, or stacked bars** (at two different times) **Stacked bars** (over a few time periods) **Surface or stacked bar** (over many time periods)	• Pie is most popular but shouldn't be! • Pie is least practical.
Item: (ranking of items) Compare rankings: same, more, less. Conversation Tip-offs: Larger than, smaller than, equal.	**Bar chart** (horizontal)	• Most versatile.
Time Series: (changes over time) See how parts change over time; does the trend increase, decrease, or stay the same? Conversation Tip-offs: change, grow, rise, decline, increase, decrease, fluctuate.	**Column chart** (vertical) **Line chart**	• Good and reliable: use a lot! • Good and reliable: use a lot!
Frequency: (items within ranges) See how many items fall into a series of progressive numerical ranges? Conversation Tip-offs: x to y range, concentration, frequency, distribution.	**Column chart** (vertical) **Line chart**	• Good and reliable: use a lot! • Good and reliable: use a lot!
Correlation: (relationship between variables) See whether relationship between two variables follows, or fails to follow, the pattern you would normally expect. Conversation Tip-offs: related to, increases with, decreases with, changes with, varies with, doesn't increase with.	**Bar chart** (horizontal) **Dot chart**	• Most versatile. • Use about 10 percent of time.

[a]Adapted from Gene Zelazny's excellent book: *Say It with Charts: The Executive's Guide to Visual Communication* (3rd ed.). Chicago: Irwin Publishing.

Bibliography

Quiñones, E. (1999, August 1). It was a dark and stormy sales pitch, and maybe it worked. *New York Times*, p. 4.

Tufte, E. R. (1990). *Envisioning Information*. Cheshire, Connecticut: Graphics Press.

Tufte, E. R. (1997). *Visual Explanations*. Cheshire, Connecticut: Graphics Press.

Zelazny, G. (1996). *Say It with Charts: The Executive's Guide to Visual Communication* (3rd ed.). Chicago: Irwin Publishing.

CHAPTER 6

Manager as Crisis Team Leader and Liaison to the Media

Your Worst Nightmare

Just a few phrases should evoke memories of the unimaginable and tragic: Bridgestone Firestone tire recall, Chernobyl explosion, Columbine High School shootings, Exxon oil spill, Love Canal toxic waste, and "mad cow" disease. This may represent a neat and tidy alphabetical listing, but no crisis is ever neat and tidy. And, to state the obvious, no crisis is wanted.

First lesson for managers:
Expect the unexpected.

Bridgestone Firestone: Recall at What Price? The House Commerce Joint Subcommittee hearing on September 6, 2000, televised on C-SPAN Live, was unsettling to watch. Representative Billy Tauzin (Commerce Consumer Protection Subcommittee Chairman), a Republican from Louisiana, led a consistently tough line of questioning. He rarely wavered from asking pointed questions. He clearly approached this opportunity to obtain testimony by asking difficult questions and redirecting questions when he (apparently) felt the answers too thin.

Representatives from Bridgestone Firestone, Ford Motor Company, State Farm Insurance, and the Highway Traffic Safety Administration (HTSA) faced difficult and probing questions. Viewers like me probably experienced a continuum of emotions from "who knew what when?" to "I'd hate to be in their shoes right now."

The Bridgestone Firestone testimony started out, for a brief time, on the offensive. Mr. Masatoshi Ono, CEO of Bridgestone Firestone, Inc., delivered his prepared statement at the beginning of his company's testimony. In part, he said:

> I am 63 years old and I have never made a public appearance like this before, so I'm more than a little bit nervous. (At this point, Mr. Ono removed his glasses and looked directly at the committee members.) As Chief Executive Officer I come before you. I apologize to you and the American peoples, especially for the family they have lost, loved ones . . . (here, Mr. Ono places his glasses on his face again.) . . . Accept full and personal responsibility on behalf of Bridgestone Firestone for the event that led to this hearing. Whenever people are hurt or . . . injured in automobile accident, it is tragic. Whenever people are injured while riding on Firestone tire(s), it is cause for the great concern among Bridgestone Firestone management and our 35,000 American employees . . .

To conclude his prepared statement, Mr. Ono cited the basic sequence of recent facts, noted that they'd already replaced nearly 2 million tires, noted that Bridgestone Firestone used competitors' tires in the replacement, and noted that his company had, in some cases, airlifted tires. He also stated that Bridgestone Firestone was actively looking for the root causes.

Mr. Ono, in my opinion, positively demonstrated his humanness by noting his nervousness. Mr. Ono, also in my opinion, looked caring when he removed his glasses and stopped reading from his prepared script for a moment; his apology seemed more credible because of this action. This author also believes that Mr. Ono's statement of "full and personal responsibility" was much needed; in fact, today's consumers demand apologies and corporate responsibility.

Second lesson for managers:
Own the problem and apologize.

The subsequent testimony of the Bridgestone Firestone executives that day, by contrast, resonated with difficulty. In fact, in some people's perceptions, the subsequent testimony conflicted with the tone first set in Mr. Ono's prepared statement.

Representative Heather Wilson, a Republican from New Mexico, initiated one such portion of testimony. Representative Wilson asked:

". . . You say that there was no defect and this is all just consumer problems and underinflation and so on. This is a, this is an internal Firestone document which I think you probably recognize. (Ms. Wilson, at this point, displayed a column graph illustrating annual rates of tire problems.) Can you tell me why it is that so many more consumers were under-inflating their tires in 1996 as opposed to other years earlier? What changed in consumer behavior?"

Representative Billy Tauzin interrupted the Bridgestone Firestone executive's answer here. Mr. Tauzin stated: "She's asking the question we should all ask. Is that because consumers were changing the inflation on their tires in one year out of all these years?" This time, the Bridgestone Firestone executive completed his answer: "No, obviously not." Mr. Tauzin continued: "No, obviously not. So why do you keep making that claim? Why do you keep telling the American public it's their fault?"

At this point, the troubled testimony looked more than difficult. The viewing audience knew that Bridgestone Firestone's list of probable causes (e.g., consumer under-inflation of tires and excessive road heat) did not match the picture told by the data on the column graph.

This author wishes this experience on no one; individuals rarely memorize all the information and data generated by a typical organization. Even well-prepared and well-meaning individuals can be forced into defensive positions during testimony—and videotaping only increases the risks.

Third lesson for managers:
Match the facts to your words and your company's actions.

Today's Reality: No Lead Time

The reality of handling crises and working with the media is that organizations have little or no lead time to analyze data in-depth and prepare intelligent on-camera responses. The central issue for organizations, unfortunately, is . . .

Prepare ahead of time for worst-case scenarios so that
you survive the real time media coverage.

This is no small task; chapters and books are now devoted to this issue (see *On Deadline: Managing Media Relations* and *Crisis in Organizations II*; full citations in this chapter's bibliography). This chapter:

1. addresses how to prepare ahead of time for worst-case scenarios in the section entitled "The Least You Need to Know"
2. covers how to survive the real-time media coverage in the section entitled "Basic Media Survival Tips"
3. offers cases upon which the readers may practice

The Least You Need to Know

People should not wait for a crisis to happen and then attempt to manage it. The excuses, on the surface, sound valid and reasonable:

- "But everyone around here is so busy. I don't really think we're in any danger, you know."
- "My company is so small. What could happen?"
- "We don't handle dangerous chemicals or anything. What would be the point of spending hours on planning for a crisis that may never happen?"

Think in these terms: It would only take one crisis and one gross mishandling of that crisis, to potentially make your company a negative focal point in the eyes of the community and in the hands of the media. What manager or business owner would want years or perhaps decades of hard work to be irreparably damaged by a singular event?

The old scouting adage, "be prepared," is good advice. As a manager, you have at least two elements to prepare in the event of a crisis: (1) the crisis communication plan, and (2) the crisis management plan. Rich Veech, the author's brother and an area administrator involved in Jefferson County Public Schools' crisis training after the tragic Columbine High School shootings, notes the simple but critical difference:

- The *crisis communication plan* covers how and when, and with whom, your team *communicates* during and after a crisis. You can prepare a preliminary plan ahead of time and then adjust the details if and when an emergency hits.
- The *crisis management plan* outlines how your team will *handle the crisis itself.* You can meet with the necessary authorities (e.g., police, fire, emergency departments, FBI, etc.) ahead of time to map out strategies and tactics for each potential kind of crisis. The Jefferson County Public School Emergency Management Plan (EMP) covers a wide range of possible events including blizzard/snow conditions; bus accidents; bomb threat; animal attack/threat; drive-by shooting; and student or staff illness, injury, or death (only naming a few potential events found in the district's materials). The bottom line, however, is that you cannot simply apply any other organization's crisis management plan to your own organization. Each organization, through its people, must create a plan that is uniquely its own.

So, what is the least you should know? The least you should know is that you cannot wait for a crisis and then think that you can *luck* your way out of it. The military, known for its preparation, is an example. You have valuable people who will depend on the company's management to lead the way during a crisis. You also have responsibilities related to your company's financial viability, and what happens during and after a crisis will affect your organization's reputation, and thus, its financial standing.

This casebook does *not* cover how to create a crisis management plan: Consult with your company's legal counsel and the appropriate authorities to create such a plan. Incident Command System (ICS) training, documented in Federal Emergency Management Agency (FEMA) materials, is offered by FEMA and some police regions. The following pages do, however, include a format for a preliminary crisis communication plan; readers are advised that they must edit this format and add to its components to make this a viable plan for their own organizations.

A Fast Start: Preliminary Crisis Communication Plan

Leaders of organizations must answer three critical and overarching questions related to crises:

1. How can we prevent potential crises?
2. How would we manage a crisis if it does occur?
3. How would we best communicate in the event of a crisis?

The answers to all three questions require proactive thinking and collaborative working relationships among organizational leaders and relevant experts such as the FBI, the police, the fire department, and emergency personnel. Collaboration can be difficult even during normal conditions; mix in the extreme emotions inherent in crises and you have a formula for potential confusion. The smartest managers plan for worst-case scenarios, hope for best-case scenarios, and work the plan if a real crisis occurs.

Rich Veech recommends:

> Think globally: It is a community endeavor. Plan with emergency management agencies in your state, county, and city. Ask yourselves questions like, "What would we do if . . . " It is incredibly difficult to make decisions (during emergencies) with a group of people. Many organizations and schools use an incident command system, similar to the fire department system. In this structure, one person is in charge. Another person handles the media management component. Another person handles communications with key stakeholders, such as employees in a company. An operations chief makes decisions regarding building and maintenance issues, for example. Another person documents all steps and activities, to maintain accurate logs and documents for legal purposes. Another person handles logistical issues such as materials and supplies. And, a separate person covers the financial and administrative issues. Preplanning is critical.

The Preliminary Crisis Communication Plan (see Table 6-1 and subsequent pages) is designed as an *advance organizer* to help you during your preplanning meetings. Use this plan to proactively think ahead. However, filling in this plan is only the first step in your overall planning. The Preliminary Crisis Communication Plan in this chapter comprises only *basic* information about *how to communicate* in the event of a crisis. This plan does *not* comprise a *crisis management plan*: Individuals from organizations must consult with the appropriate authorities to plan how they will handle an actual crisis (i.e., developing the crisis management plan) in their area. The author recommends that you consult other resources and experts to create a complete crisis management plan for your organization.

The author recommends that readers review the Bibliography at the end of this chapter for a short list of additional resources. The author further recommends that organizational leaders must consult with the appropriate authorities when planning and handling crisis management strategies and tactics.

See Laurence Barton's *Crisis in Organizations: II*—Appendix A contains a crisis management plan template and Appendix B lists crisis Web resources (full citation in the bibliography for this chapter).

TABLE 6-1   Preliminary Crisis Communication Plan

(This document helps you jump-start your crisis communications planning process; it does *not* comprise a complete communications plan *nor* does it comprise a crisis management plan.
Add action steps, lists, and information to build your plans.)
Three potential scenarios that could place us at greatest risk (in one or two sentences):

(Laurence Barton, in *Crisis in Organizations II*, suggests that there are three categories of risks: those that impact *people, financial conditions*, or *company reputation. It may help to think about the top three risks that could occur under each category and organize a one-page list such as this.*

People Risk 1:

People Risk 2:

People Risk 3:

Financial Risk 1:

Financial Risk 2:

Financial Risk 3:

Reputation Risk 1:

Reputation Risk 2:

Reputation Risk 3:

TABLE 6-1   *(continued)*

Core Crisis Team Members:

Crisis Leader:*	Second in Command:*
Name:	Name
Job title:	Job Title:
Location:	Location:
Work phone:	Work phone:
Home phone:	Home phone:
Cell phone:	Cell phone:
Other phone:	Other phone:
Pager:	Pager:
E-mail:	E-mail:
Fax:	Fax:
Other critical info:	Other critical info:
Assistant's name, phone, e-mail, location:	Assistant's name, phone, e-mail, location:

Note: The Crisis Leader works with the Core Crisis Team members to oversee all media interactions and approve communications to stakeholders.

Note: The Second in Command could be designated as the official spokesperson with the media (this alleviates some pressure from the Crisis Leader

Legal Counsel:	*Others TBD:* *(Technical experts, information technology head, etc.)*
Name:	Name
Job title:	Job Title:
Location:	Location:
Work phone:	Work phone:
Home phone:	Home phone:
Cell phone:	Cell phone:
Other phone:	Other phone:
Pager:	Pager:
E-mail:	E-mail:
Fax:	Fax:
Other critical info:	Other critical info:
Assistant's name, phone, e-mail, location:	Assistant's name, phone, e-mail, location

PRELIMINARY CRISIS COMMUNICATION PLAN—ADVANCE CHECKLIST

Does the Core Crisis Team have *at least* the following prepared in advance of a potential crisis?

Crisis Management Strategy:
- Has the Core Crisis Team met with the appropriate federal, state, county, and city agencies (e.g., FBI, police, fire, emergency personnel) to plan how to effectively handle any specific crises that might occur in this specific organization?
- Has the Core Crisis Team developed specific crisis action plans prior to any potential crises—separate action plans to cover different kinds of incidents?
- Has the Core Crisis Team ensured that managers and employees at all locations are trained (e.g., how to handle emergencies, whom to refer the media to, procedures, etc.) prior to any potential crises?
- Have strategies and tactical plans been developed for all organizational locations?
- Does the Core Crisis Team regularly update the Preliminary Communication Plan to ensure accuracy of all contact names and numbers?

Bottom Line Strategy:
- A list of statements *not* to say/behaviors *not* to demonstrate (e.g., don't communicate names of victims until official procedures are completed and families have been notified; don't respond in anger to reporter's question)?
- A visual timeline or flowchart of key events (as brainstormed during proactive troubleshooting planning sessions) with space for responding to real-time/unforeseen events?

People/Facility Locations:
- Names, contact info, and bios on all key executives and managers related to risk scenario?
- Geographic maps, facility floor plans, etc., for all potentially affected sites?
- Employee population and basic demographic information for all potentially affected sites?

Command Central/Emergency Info:
- Designated *command central* location (e.g., with phones, computers, printers, paper, fax, television, radio; sleeping and rest room facilities; conference tables, overhead projector, flip charts, markers, etc.)?
- Secondary command central location with alternative communication capabilities (if first location is unavailable)?
- Names and contact information for police, fire department, ambulance service, hospitals, and other relevant emergency crews?
- Agent's name and contact information for insurance company?

Legal Counsel and Psychological Assistance:
- Names and contact information for company's legal counsel?
- Relevant information on recent events or similar scenarios?
- Names and contact information for psychologists familiar with your specific culture?

External / Media Relations:
- Names and contact information for members of media?
- Instructions for employees regarding directing media questions to authorized company leaders?

Internal Communications:
- List of *go to* managers (people trusted to disseminate approved information to internal employees)?
- Approved information and master schedule for disseminating information?

Personal Needs:
- Change of clothes, overnight kits?
- Sources for meals to be delivered to command central?
- Sources for close proximity lodging?

PRELIMINARY CRISIS COMMUNICATION PLAN—PREPARED STATEMENT

Keep a first draft of a prepared statement on file (see Table 6-2); fill in the appropriate details if and when a crisis occurs. Many companies also maintain a "dark site" on their Website: details are added if a crisis occurs and the dark site is activated for use by the media and other stakeholders.

TABLE 6-2 Sample Prepared Statement

Potential Scenario:	*Immediate Central Message to Communicate:* *(cover the who, what, when, where, why, and how)*
Example: Potential people risk 1: Power plant explosion	(Cover the *who, what, when, where*) An explosion occurred at ____ this afternoon at our ____ location. A fire resulted.
	(Cover *how* we're handling scenario) Our management is on site and we are working with the emergency crews.
	(Emphasize that we *care*) Everyone in our organization is extremely concerned about this situation and every individual involved. Our first concern is our people.
	(Revisit *how* we're handling scenario) We will work around the clock until the situation is fully contained; our chief executive officer is en route as we speak.
	(State that we will look for *why*) After the immediate danger is over, we will investigate to find the cause of the explosion and take precautions to a similar situation in the future.
	(Reach out to community in an *interactive* way. People will feel a need to regain some control so give them a vehicle to take some small action) If families and friends have questions, please call this 800 number.

PRELIMINARY CRISIS COMMUNICATION PLAN—AFFECTED GROUPS AND THE INFORMATION THEY NEED

See Table 6-3 for sample preliminary verbage from communicating with various groups.

TABLE 6-3 Groups and Suggested Messages	
Potential Stakeholder Groups Affected: (Brainstorm a list of all groups that might be affected by potential risks)	*Key Message Needed, by Group:* (Keep first draft messages on file; fill in the appropriate details if and when a crisis occurs.)
Families/friends/community citizens	Announce phone number(s) or an 800 number: to obtain information on status of emergency, safety of general worker population, rescue operations, and designated hospitals.
	Announce safe place to congregate, to await further news, and to support each other.
Plant employees	Provide central number(s): for shift workers to learn whether or not to report to work; to learn status of emergency, safety of general worker population, rescue operations, and designated hospitals; to identify meeting place, if necessary.
	Announce safe place to congregate, to await further news, and to support each other.
Media	(See "Preliminary Crisis Communication Plan—Sample Prepared Statement" section)
Others	

Basic Media Survival Tips

Do you have the basic instincts to survive these scenarios? Instructions:

1. *Identify what is wrong* with each statement or action in Box 6-1.
2. *Explain why* the statement or action is problematic. Discuss the potential consequences and/or how others might perceive each manager.
3. *Rephrase* each statement or *alter* the action to preserve the manager's credibility.

SPEAKING WITH REPORTERS

Remember these steps when preparing to speak with reporters.

Plan Ahead

- Identify, by name, the people designated to speak with the media. Inform your entire organization that only those people are authorized to issue formal statements. Cultivate media relationships prior to a crisis.
- Speak simply if you want to be quoted correctly. Speak in long sentences and "think out loud" if you want to increase your chances of being *mis*quoted: Don't force reporters to paraphrase for you.
- Practice with a cross-functional team. Imagine worst-case scenarios and media questions, then brainstorm to formulate well-worded answers.

| BOX 6-1 |

Scenarios

1. The manager says to the interviewer, "Thanks for having me."

2. A manager says to the reporter, "I don't understand the question."

3. A manager says to a reporter, "I don't know the answer to that question. Next question, please."

4. A manager wears a tweed jacket for an on-camera interview.

5. A manager wears an open-neck collar during an on-camera interview.

6. A company spokesperson looks away when answering on-camera interview questions.

7. An official company statement notes that a product problem will affect only a small percentage of customers.

8. A manager refuses powder on his/her face prior to an on-camera interview.

9. Manager C., an enthusiastic personality, does not tone down her animated facial expressions and gestures for an on-camera interview.

10. Manager Y., during a long-distance, split-screen television interview, is pitted against another interviewee with a diverging opinion. During the other interviewee's Q&A, Manager Y rolls her eyes, shakes her head, and generally looks disapproving.

See Table 6-4 for sample solutions to these scenarios.

Start with a Simple Goal

- Use an analogy or metaphor. The visual story created through your analogy or metaphor often causes reporters to use *your* words. Your analogies or metaphors may be more flattering than the ones created by reporters.
- Remember that different rules apply during interviews. Speak with the purpose of providing succinct information as opposed to engaging in a conversation. Remember the witness-stand rule: Answer succinctly, remain silent, and wait for the next question.
- Focus on a central idea when a crisis hits. Prior to speaking with the media, prepare a central idea with related statements and answers to support that central idea. For example, "We are dedicated to seeing this through."

Don't Play Games

- Don't avoid the press as a strategy. Your hiding behaviors raise their suspicions (and the suspicions of the public).
- Avoid "no comment" like the plague. If you don't provide information, then don't expect a fair portrayal. Do you want reporters to rely on primary sources (e.g., you) or secondary sources (e.g., anyone)? You probably don't want to read that you or your company "refused to respond to our requests for comment." "No comment" simply raises suspicions.
- Don't feel that you must answer hypothetical questions. Stick to the facts and state that you are doing so. For example, "I won't guess about a hypothetical situation. Let me say again . . . "

- Don't fill in blank spaces. When interviewers pause, they often want you to talk and perhaps provide them with an unfortunate quotable quote. Again, remember the witness-stand rule: Answer succinctly, remain silent, and wait for the next question.
- Stick to the facts. Give succinct answers; leave out a few details if necessary, but never lie. Credibility is vital to your success, so don't blow it.
- Don't come out fighting when your back is against a wall. If you must admit an error, pair the facts with clearly stated action steps designed to alleviate the error. Add that your company dedicates future actions toward avoiding a similar error.

Table 6-4 contains sample solutions to Box 6-1 scenarios.

TABLE 6-4   Sample Solutions

Rephrased Statement/Altered Action	*Why You Would Want the Change*
1. "Thank you."	Unfortunately, double meanings bring an unwanted sexual connotation to the phrase "Thank you for having me." Also, the original wording could be confusing to English-as-a-second-language listeners.
2. "Please rephrase the question."	Avoid "I don't understand . . ." because it might place a negative and unwarranted focus on the manager's expertise or ability.
3. "I will get the answer to that question for you as soon as possible. We need to gather more information."	Avoid "I don't know . . ." because it might put the manager's expertise or ability into question. However, you could say, "I don't know about that particular situation" if asked about an incident about which you have no knowledge.
4. Wear a solid color jacket.	Tweed jackets visually appear to vibrate on film.
5. Wear a shirt with a collar that is buttoned close to the neck.	An open-neck collar makes many people look too casual or unkempt on camera.
6. Look directly at the interviewer or into the camera.	Looking away results in viewers worrying about your honesty.
7. Apologize for the inconvenience to customers and state how you will fix the problem.	When you say only a few will be affected, those few feel unimportant to your company. You risk losing their business.
8. Accept the powder.	Faces shine too much on camera when they lack powder. (Candidate Richard Nixon refused powder before his debate with John Kennedy. Nixon's face glistened with sweat during the broadcast.)
9. Restrict facial gestures and keep gestures within the camera's view.	If you don't tone it down, you'll look foolish on-camera because the camera exaggerates everything. Also, if you nod while listening to a question, viewers might read this as implied agreement with the reporter's question.
10. Listen calmly when another person talks.	You'll be judged as credible if you maintain professional composure; you'll be perceived as childish if you make faces.

CASES

Case 6-1 Communication Plan (Media Focus)

(Case purpose: Create a communication plan for handling the media.)

STEP 1: REVIEW THE BIG PICTURE

This case focuses on an organization in trouble: This company must reduce product lines, close plants, and lay off people. If this organization mishandles internal and external communications, managers face unnecessary conflict and mistrust. See Case 7-4, "Communication Plan (Internal Focus)," in Chapter 7, for how to create two related documents: the company president's announcement speech and a corporate-wide work plan to handle all communication steps.

Background

Alpha Beta (AB) Computers is a hardware/software company in operation for approximately 13 years and with 18 product lines. AB's world headquarters is in Chicago; 120 managers and 1,280 employees are distributed among the executive, design, sales, and marketing divisions. There are 10 manufacturing and distribution points in the United States: three in the eastern region (total employee population is 750), one in the Midwestern region (population is 250), two in the southern region (population is 527), and four in the western region (population is 1,710).

Current Status

The distribution chain includes value-add resellers (VARs) with 95 percent of the business), and AB-only retail comprising 5 percent of the business. The sales managers ($n = 2000$) and sales representatives ($n =$ approximately 17,000; in constant turnover) are the target audiences for the product knowledge and sales incentives programs driven by corporate. Two computer companies are rapidly encroaching on the market share and AB's profits have dropped by 12 percent in the last quarter. Overall profitability and sales volume trends are also on a downswing.

Wave One of the President's Strategy

The company president decided that consolidating from 18 to 12 product lines is the first wave of attack against the issues facing the company. The hardware lines won't change; however, revamped software lines will eliminate redundancies and slow features (as identified through customer satisfaction data). Any software with a poor sales performance record is in jeopardy.

Wave Two of the President's Strategy

The company president made a difficult decision to downsize within the next 6 months (less time is better). The downsizing will be positioned as the second wave of attack against the company's problems. One manufacturing and distribution point in the east and one in the south will close. Head count will drop by 350 in the east (because of the Long Island closing) and by 275 in the south (the Atlanta site is closing). Remaining sites in the east and south will pick up the slack (i.e., take over the work).

Assume that you are the consulting team assigned to AB Computers; AB executives called in your team because of an unforeseen problem. In the midst of AB Computers' plans to implement the downsizing, plant closing, and product consolidation, the media prematurely contacted AB's president (several messages were left with the president's secretary between 8:00 A.M. and 10:30 A.M. this morning).

AB had scheduled a 1:00 P.M. presidential speech to all employees, this afternoon. Unfortunately, the media heard about the changes before the president's scheduled announcement. (You wonder if AB Computers, perhaps, has a mole providing the media with confidential information.)

It is now 11:45 A.M. and your consulting team is in AB's executive conference room. AB's executives are worried. Your response to the media must be immediate. Representatives of AB Computers must answer the reporters' questions as truthfully as possible: The company is known for its integrity. Also, the accurate information leaked to the press makes it indefensible to delay responding to the media.

Your consulting team's current task is threefold:

1. Create a *media management strategy*. Answer the following questions to help you generate ideas for your strategy:
   - Will you select a specific company spokesperson? If yes, which job title would be represented by that person? Would you rehearse before greeting the media? Will you include a media "answer" that tells reporters how to get accurate information in the future, or will you ignore this information leak when you speak with reporters?
   - Will you provide truthful answers but without all the details, or will you tell the media everything since they seem to know so much, anyway? Also, will you inform management and employees to respond to media contacts, or will you tell AB people to channel all requests for interviews and information through a specific corporate executive?
2. Script *answers to the sample media questions* in Box 6-2 (these questions are not in sequential or priority order). Always focus answers around a central idea and begin each answer with the bottom line so that the media is more likely to use the answers you want them to.
3. If desired, brainstorm other potential questions and answers (based on your experience or creative thought).

BOX 6-2

Sample Media Questions

1. After AB Computer's wonderful history, why do you have to close two plants now?

2. Exactly how many people will be fired? (Note to AB's spokesperson: Watch the terminology—"fired" is quite different than "laid off.")

3. You will lose many valuable employees to the competition, won't you? (Note to AB's spokesperson: Don't feel as though you must repeat the question as part of your answer. Why give free advertising time to your competitors? Answer the question without mentioning your competition.)

4. Aren't your executives concerned about the economic health of Long Island and Atlanta if you close those two plants?

5. Accountability is a big issue these days. How is AB Computers accountable for the loss of jobs?

6. Your competitors say that your new product line will confuse customers. What do you say? (Note to AB's spokesperson: Don't repeat the words "confuse customers" in your answer. Focus on how the streamlined product line will help your customers make decisions.)

7. Off the record, can you tell me if this is the beginning of more widespread layoffs? (Note to AB's spokesperson: Nothing is "off the record." Be careful!)

8. Someone in your organization leaked the information about the plant closings. One of your employees says that everyone in your company is angry at this point. Can you tell me if this is true? (Note to AB's spokesperson: If you criticize this "one employee" on the air, you'll look bad. Also, don't defend alleged widespread opinions; instead, focus on positive employee activities that can be proven.)

9. Let me ask you a hypothetical question: What if your sales drop over the next quarter—then what will you do? (Note to AB's spokesperson: Beware of hypothetical questions. Most experts tell you to decline to answer a hypothetical question and immediately return to your central message.)

10. We have 30 seconds to wrap up. What do you want the Long Island and Atlanta communities to know at this point? (Note to AB's spokesperson: Don't let the time constraint throw you. Return to your central message, state concern for the people in these communities, and explain what your company is doing to assist people during the transition.)

11. Oh, come on now! Do you really expect these communities to believe that your company could not avoid the layoffs? (Note to AB's spokesperson: Don't let the interviewer's disbelieving wording bother you. State your answer in the positive.)

12. So what you're saying is that AB Computers is in trouble and that these two plants are just the first two to be closed? (Note to AB's spokesperson: Be cautious of paraphrased questions that do not reflect what you've said. Don't repeat the question; instead, state your answer succinctly without repeating the scare tactic wording of " . . . are just the first two to be closed.")

(*continued*)

Box 6-2 (*continued*)

13. So, what you're doing is firing valuable employees and keeping all of your senior managers? (Note to AB's spokesperson: First, you are not firing people, you are laying off people. Second, don't make a distinction between employees and managers; state that the leadership needed to move the company forward is in place.)

14. So, about 600 of your people are being laid off, right? (Note to AB's spokesperson: Unless you are ready to announce exact numbers, avoid it for now.)

15. Can you say that, frankly, this is just the first step in a larger strategic plan to reorganize your company? (Note to AB's spokesperson: Don't repeat words such as "frankly" in your answer.)

16. I have heard that women are more likely to be laid off, without chances for transfers to your other plants, than are men. Is this true? (Note to AB's spokesperson: Consult your legal counsel as you rehearse potential questions and answers. You'd want advice on this kind of question.)

17. Isn't this really just an economic decision? (Note to AB's spokesperson: You must emphasize your concern for people; don't fall into the trap of talking only dollars and sounding uncaring as a result.)

18. What is the key message you're sending to consumers with this reorganization?

19. Won't your new product line confuse buyers? (Note to AB's spokesperson: Focus on fewer and better products.)

20. Off the record, don't these changes in your company disturb you? (Note to AB's spokesperson: There is no "off the record," and don't repeat the word "disturb.")

21. I have a memo here, dated 1 year ago, written by your company's CFO. It says that economic indicators are not strong and our profits continue to decline. Why wasn't something done a year ago? (Note to AB's spokesperson: This question requires legal counsel. Don't lie. Most company spokespersons in this situation could say that analysis and planning efforts have been going on for some time.)

22. Why did your executive team just return from a weekend retreat in the mountains if you are now laying off several hundred people? (Note to AB's spokesperson: Emphasize their analysis and planning work and de-emphasize the location.)

STEP 2: ANALYZE FACTS AND EMOTIONS (F&Es)

AB's executive team, and the consultants, should first ask a series of *what if* questions to help them create their strategy. For example, what would happen if:

1. AB doesn't respond today to the reporters, and the media broadcasts this news without including AB's perspective?
2. AB employees hear the news from the media before they hear it as an official message from AB management?
3. Someone within AB, not designated by management, speaks with the media?

These questions, alone, create a call for action and honesty. Review the sample strategy in Tables 6-5 and 6-6.

STEP 3: DESIGN THE STRATEGY

TABLE 6-5 Media Management Strategy

Avoid an emotional response.	Don't waste precious meeting time wondering who the mole might be; worry about that later.
Manage the media logistics first.	Designate an official representative to return the reporters' calls. Tell the reporters that AB's president will meet with them at 1:30 P.M. today (following the president's speech to all employees). Give reporters enough lead time to write accurate and complete stories; hold this session as early in the day as you can. Select an appropriate location on company grounds rather than the president's office.
Manage your employees' concerns as planned.	You cannot talk to the media before you inform your own people. Proceed with your speech, as planned, at 1:00 P.M. today. (Headquarters people attend in the auditorium. Field offices and plant locations view via videoconference.)
Manage the outflow of information.	Review and edit the president's speech draft to ensure that the wording reflects the right message.
	Contact key executives and managers to ensure that they do not answer any media questions.
	Add a line to the president's speech (especially if this point has not been clearly communicated to all employees): "All information to the media will go through me (the president) or our vice president of communications. If reporters contact you, refer them to our official spokesperson, the vice president of communications (name here)."
	Note: Incorporate these instructions in written form (e.g., e-mail and/or memo) to all employees, as well.
Organize your media response.	Organize the reporters' questions (from the morning voice mail) by theme (e.g., questions about people, AB's finances, AB's reputation, products, etc.). Cross-reference the president's speech.
	Brainstorm other questions that could be asked.
	Script simple, honest answers to the questions (collaborative process between the executive and consultant teams).
	Rehearse the president and vice president of communications on how to best phrase answers (see Table 6-6). Plan a *central idea* around which to focus your message.

TABLE 6-6 Responses to a Few of the Sample Media Questions

After AB Computer's wonderful history, why do you have to close two plants now?	AB Computers holds a strong position in our industry. Every organization goes through change, and our time for change is now. We've listened to our customers and it is time for change: Users of AB Computers want fewer products that work faster.
Exactly how many people will be fired?	(Don't repeat the word *fired* in your answer!)
	We continue to change to meet customer needs; this is simply our most significant evolution to date. We, sadly, must close the Atlanta and Long Island plants; we will help approximately 625 people look for other jobs in AB Computers or with other companies.
Aren't your executives concerned about the economic health of Long Island and Atlanta if you close those two plants?	AB Computers, in collaboration with an outstanding outplacement firm, will help people look for other suitable employment in those communities.
Accountability is a big issue these days. How is AB Computers accountable for the loss of jobs?	Every organization goes through change and our time for change is now. The management team of AB Computers analyzes critical competitive data and evaluates all options for change. We will continue to thoroughly review all steps in our strategic plan.
Your competitors say that your new product line will confuse customers. What do you say?	(Don't repeat the word *confuse* in your answer!)
	Our loyal customers have asked for these changes. AB Computers has smart customers: They want fewer products that work faster.
Off the record, can you tell me if this is the beginning of more widespread layoffs?	AB Computers is a strong organization with valued products. These evolutionary changes now position us for a bright competitive future.

Case 6-2 Macro Planning Positive News Coverage

(Case purpose: Proactively generate strategically positioned news stories.)

STEP 1: REVIEW THE BIG PICTURE

For this case, assume that you are in charge of media relations for a large, well-established company. Your company's 100-year anniversary occurs 7 months from now (i.e., during "month 6" of the calendar timeline in Step 3 of this case) and executive management wants to take full advantage of this event. Your organization suffered negative media coverage 5 months ago when you pulled a major product from retail shelves: Consumer safety was not at issue, but the product's defect rendered your product ineffective. Your company lost many thousands of dollars recalling the product, fixing the design issue, and trying to regain consumer faith in your product line.

Your executive team (representing all functional areas of your organization) agrees that smart media strategic planning would greatly enhance consumer awareness of your brand and could also reposition your company's reputation in the market. The team wants "6 months of positive media blitz" leading up to the extravagant anniversary party planned 7 months from this month. You just left a meeting in which the group brainstormed many positive activities and events that might be included in such a positive media blitz. A few people in the group also generated specific ideas for how to communicate with the media. Your team will now prepare a high-level calendar prior to your next executive team meeting so that everyone can see the proposed sequence of events at a glance.

Your tasks are to:

1. Select an industry, a company name, and a product line that sells via retail for the purposes of the case.
2. Review the preliminary list of events generated from the brainstorm (Box 6-3) related to the company anniversary, your product line, employee programs, and community involvement activities. Assign *target dates* for these events to occur (*don't* document the up-front planning time or activities required to move the events toward the target dates).
3. Review the list of events and create additional ideas for newsworthy items.
4. Plot the list of events on a generic planning calendar (there is no need to identify a specific number of days in any given month at this stage of your planning).

Focus on maintaining the momentum throughout the entire 6-month period. Think from the consumers' point of view: Consider what consumers might see and hear via the media, and when they would receive this information over your 6-month window of time. What would consumers need to know first about the quality of your product line? What might pique their interest about your company's philosophy and people? What could change or positively enhance their perceptions about your company and your product line?

STEP 2: ANALYZE FACTS AND EMOTIONS (F&Es)

Facts

You must use the key events and ideas already generated on the brainstorm list. You are, however, not limited to this list. You'll gain an added value from this case if you generate ideas beyond the list provided in this casebook. If you can learn to consistently see opportunities in difficult or "business as usual" times rather than seeing barriers, then you have a better chance of evoking positive consumer behavior. Some might call this *spin*. However, every company must ride the upward and downward cycles and manage those trend lines toward a positive goal: No company escapes this life cycle.

Emotions

People, in their haste to plan, often drop to a detailed level far too early in their thinking and discussions—especially people who dislike working by committee or people

BOX 6-3

Preliminary List of Events

(List generated from brainstorm and *not* arranged in sequential order or by stakeholder category.)

- Open new child-care centers (facilities now being built at world headquarters and the 15 plants around the country, centers due to open 14 months from now).
- Organize online opportunities (e.g., chat rooms, Web site advertising, and white papers).
- Organize employee volunteer groups at Habitat for Humanity house-building events.
- Finalize new services for retirees (e.g., special rates on banking, regional vacation spots near headquarters and the 15 plants).
- Arrange for satisfied customer testimonials to be included in advertising.
- Plan executive and plant management speeches at local and regional meetings (e.g., chambers of commerce, women management groups, young presidents organizations).
- Hold 100-year anniversary parties planned at world headquarters and our 15 plants in U.S. and Canada.
- Offer reduced rates for teenage children of employees to health clubs and regional sporting events.
- Deliver quality control training at all plants.
- Plan at least two relevant articles for industry-specific journals.
- Announce that company president is to win Distinguished Business Leader Award

(given from the city in which world headquarters is located, award dinner slated for month 3 of overall media blitz timeline).

- Announce that customer satisfaction data proves that customers are increasingly happy with all of our products (in spite of the recently recalled product). (Scores are gradually rising, based on calls made to customers receiving replacement product.).
- Combine 100-year anniversary celebration theme with trade show exhibits (to begin during month 4 of 6-month timeline).
- Make special announcements to stockholders.
- Create a list of frequently asked questions (FAQs) about the 100-year company history (provide to media as part of media blitz).
- Distribute frequently asked questions (FAQs) about the 100-year company history to sales division, customer service department, all managers, and employees—formats for each population to be determined.
- Offer product giveaways through media personalities (e.g., note the product reviews and product giveaways on shows like *Oprah*).
- Send celebration peripherals to headquarters and plant locations (e.g., banners, "good news" announcements).
- Hold news conference and anniversary reception.

who don't like to waste time. Don't fall into this strategic planning trap. Yes, you've generated a list of tactics. However, your task now is to create a big picture look at a 6-month strategy.

Your team, at this point in the planning process, must maintain a high-level, "40,000-foot view." Your team, during this stage of planning, cannot focus on details. For example, if your team gets bogged down in arguing over specific dates, then you significantly slow your process and stifle your creativity. Therefore, use the generic planning calendar on the subsequent pages and avoid things like, "The third month in our window of opportunity has 31 days" or "That month has 5 weeks, not 4."

Your team must also maintain a narrow focus on the employee and consumer points of view. First, internal integrity is crucial. You cannot plan events or messages that engender mistrust in your own people. In other words, your company cannot, in essence, say one thing and do another. You have to treat your employees, on a daily basis, as well as you say you do in media messages. Second, external integrity is critical. Your company's consumer trust was recently shaken by the product recall. Think about the following questions:

- How can you position every event as a statement about how people can trust the organization, your people, and your product?
- What would the publicized events say about your organization's integrity, credibility, and trust?
- Have you first gained true employee buy-in before publicizing events to the general public (e.g., don't widely publicize a volunteer effort if employees feel coerced to help or if only a tiny percentage of the employee population participate)?

STEP 3: DESIGN THE STRATEGY

First, organize the ideas by stakeholder categories to determine if any critical stakeholder groups have been neglected (see Table 6-7).

Plan your activities for the next 8 months (see Tables 6-8 through 6-15) beginning with month "zero," the month before the media blitz starts. Inform your own first: In month "zero" you focus first on making your employees and the retail establishments fully aware of your company's good news. Then, the efforts can expand to other stakeholders.

TABLE 6-7 Stakeholder Groups

Stakeholder Group	Idea (from Brainstorm)
Customers	• Announce that customer satisfaction data proves that customers are increasingly happy with our products.
Retail establishments	• Announce that customer satisfaction data proves that customers are increasingly happy with our products.
Employees	• Announce that customer satisfaction data proves that customers are increasingly happy with our products. • Deliver quality control training at all plants. • Distribute FAQs to sales, customer service, managers, and employees. • Send celebration peripherals to HQ and plants (e.g., banners). • Hold news conference and anniversary reception.
Employees and Families	• Open new child-care centers. • Finalize new services for retirees. • Hold 100-year anniversary parties at HQ and plants. • Offer reduced rates for teenage children of employees to health clubs and regional sporting events.
Communities	• Organize employee volunteer groups (e.g., Habitat for Humanity). • Plan executive and plant management speeches at local and regional meetings (e.g., chambers of commerce).
Stockholders	• Make special announcements to stockholders.
Industry	• Plan at least two relevant articles for industry-specific journals. • Combine 100-year anniversary celebration theme with trade show exhibits.
General public	• Organize online opportunities. • Arrange for satisfied customer testimonials in advertising. • Create a list of FAQs about the 100-year company history (provide to media as part of media blitz). • Offer product giveaways through media personalities.
Media (Include because the media influences how others perceive your company.)	• Arrange for satisfied customer testimonials in advertising. • Offer product giveaways through media personalities. • Hold news conference and anniversary reception.
All groups	• Announce that company president is to win Distinguished Business Leader Award.

TABLE 6-8 Month "Zero"

Key message (central idea for media blitz):
Message will vary depending upon industry, company, and product selected by reader.

Week 1	Inform employees (e.g., via company newsletter, memos, and department meetings) that customer satisfaction is improving; emphasize key message and how employees can impact customer satisfaction. Complete quality control training at all plants during this month.
Week 2	Include information about improving customer satisfaction with mailers and during manufacturer representative visits to retail locations.
Week 3	Distribute FAQs to sales, customer service, managers, and employees.
Week 4	Include information about why products satisfy customers in mailers or e-mail announcements to customers.

TABLE 6-9	Month 1
Week 1	Provide a list of FAQs about the 100-year company history (as media blitz begins); include relevant photographs that the media can use in their stories.
Week 2	Release online opportunities (e.g., chat rooms, Web site advertising, and white papers).
Week 3	Deliver executive or plant management speech at local or regional meeting (e.g., chamber of commerce).
Week 4	Deliver executive or plant management speech at local or regional meeting (e.g., chamber of commerce).

TABLE 6-10	Month 2
Week 1	Release advertising that includes satisfied customer testimonials.
Week 2	Offer product giveaways through media personalities (e.g., local news shows, shows like *Oprah*); continue every month.
Week 3	Deliver executive or plant management speech at local or regional meeting (e.g., chamber of commerce).
Week 4	Announce that company president is to win Distinguished Business Leader award (during month 3 of this timeline).

TABLE 6-11	Month 3
Week 1	Distribute press release announcing company president's Distinguished Business Leader Award.
Week 2	Send executive delegation to award dinner for company president as he or she wins Distinguished Business Leader Award.
	Hold company reception for employees and president to celebrate president's Distinguished Business Leader Award.
Week 3	Offer product giveaways through media personalities (e.g., local news shows, or shows like *Oprah*); continue every month.
Week 4	Deliver executive or plant management speech at local or regional meeting (e.g., chamber of commerce).

TABLE 6-12	Month 4
Week 1	Combine 100-year anniversary celebration theme with trade show exhibits.
	Organize employee volunteer groups (e.g., Habitat for Humanity) and distribute press release about their efforts.
Week 2	Release article in industry-specific journal.
Week 3	Deliver executive or plant management speech at local or regional meeting (e.g., chamber of commerce).
Week 4	Offer product giveaways through media personalities (e.g., local news shows, shows like *Oprah*); continue every month.

TABLE 6-13	Month 5
Week 1	Send celebration peripherals to headquarters and plants (e.g., banners). Make special announcements to stockholders (e.g., related to customer satisfaction and 100-year anniversary).
Week 2	Deliver executive or plant management speech at local or regional meeting (e.g., chamber of commerce).
Week 3	Announce new services for retirees (e.g., mailers to retirees and press release to media).
Week 4	Offer product giveaways through media personalities (e.g., local news shows, shows like *Oprah*); continue every month.

TABLE 6-14	Month 6
Week 1	Hold news conference and a formal anniversary reception (invite employees, retirees, and the media). Hold 100-year anniversary parties at HQ and plants (small parties held all month). Offer reduced rates for teenage children of employees to health clubs and regional sporting events.
Week 2	Release article in industry-specific journal.
Week 3	Deliver executive or plant management speech at local or regional meeting (e.g., chamber of commerce).
Week 4	Offer product giveaways through media personalities (e.g., local news shows, shows like *Oprah*); continue every month.

TABLE 6-15	Month 6, Plus One
	(What is your strategy after the 6-month media blitz ends?)
Week 1	Prepare informational review of recent events and news coverage for internal management and employees (perhaps to publish in company newsletter).
Week 2	Offer product giveaways through media personalities (e.g., local news shows, shows like *Oprah*); continue every month.
Week 3	Solicit feedback and evaluative comments from key managers involved in recent events, use opinions and comments to organize future events and proactive news coverage.
Week 4	Distribute press release regarding upcoming opening of new child-care centers.

Case 6-3 Questionable Practices

(Case purpose: Handle the media during an investigation into an executive's behavior.)

STEP 1: REVIEW THE BIG PICTURE

In this case, you are the vice president of communications for a multinational corporation. A news story just broke this afternoon about an alleged case of sexual harassment brought by a female employee against one of your executives. The reporters find this event newsworthy because several women in your organization have apparently come forward publicly to say that they were harassed, as well. In fact, the women named not one, but three, of your company's executives as offenders.

It is 4:45 P.M. and you just left a series of internal meetings with corporate legal counsel and the executive team. At this point, internal investigations have just begun. As you leave the headquarters building and try to enter your car, several reporters (with cameras rolling) approach you. The reporters' questions range from "Are the sexual harassment allegations true?" to "Is it true that your organization has covered up widespread sexual harassment for years?"

Your task: Explain *how* you would respond, and explain *why* you would select such a strategy.

STEP 2: ANALYZE FACTS AND EMOTIONS (F&Es)

The facts in this case exist at two levels:

1. Facts for external consumption: The media already knows something. Therefore, a response of "no comment" would only make the viewing and reading public suspicious of you and your organization. The media needs to know something, but their "need to know" does not equate to sharing full information at this point.
2. Facts for internal consumption: Your organization is currently conducting an internal investigation. Therefore, you cannot compromise those proceedings by giving too much information at this point. Also, you cannot release information to the media before the people within your organization hear it from you and your executive team.

Your emotions, at this point, may range anywhere along a continuum. For example:

- It has been a long day; I'm tired and I don't want to answer any questions.
- I'm not yet authorized to release information; anything I say may get me in trouble.
- Why was I the first to leave the building? I should have followed the CEO out.
- Whatever I say tonight will be seen and read by our managers and employees. If what I say is misinterpreted, I then have to field calls tomorrow from our own people as well as the media. I can't win here.

STEP 3: DESIGN THE STRATEGY

Now, to return to the scenario: The reporters' questions range from "Are the sexual harassment allegations true?" to "Is it true that your organization has covered up widespread sexual harassment for years?"

You might respond by saying (as you unlock your car door and open it): "We are now in the process of conducting a thorough investigation. Since the lives and careers of all people involved are important to us, we will not release any details at this time. We take these allegations seriously. We will resolve the situation as quickly and fairly as possible."

What is your emotional reaction to this response? Can you improve on this response—would you add to it, or delete or change any part of it? What other responses might be appropriate in this case?

Case 6-4   Product Recall
(Case purpose: Develop a product recall strategy to communicate to the public.)

STEP 1: REVIEW THE BIG PICTURE

For the purposes of this case, you sit on the external relations committee for a small watch manufacturing company. Most of your product is sold, at least for now, within the Midwest. A woman's sports watch was recently redesigned and released into production 6 months ago; however, it is clearly defective. Your research and development department worked with the customer relations department to ferret through consumer complaints and product return data. Several reports have been delivered to senior management; as the data grew, everyone agreed that your team could no longer delay a decision. The unfortunate conclusion is that, while there is no danger to consumers, you must now recall the watches.

Your task: Your committee is responsible for developing a *recall strategy*. What *methods and media* will you use to announce the recall? What *internal procedures* will you establish to handle the increased volume of retail and consumer calls and e-mails?

STEP 2: ANALYZE FACTS AND EMOTIONS (F&Es)

The facts are simple:

- You must recall the watch.
- Your customers are not in physical danger because of the recall.
- Your customers will be inconvenienced by the recall.
- You risk losing newer, less loyal customers if the recall is mismanaged.
- You risk angering established, more loyal customers if the recall is mismanaged.

The emotions, when viewed from the perspectives of the various stakeholders, require a bit of strategic planning:

- Senior management worries about recall costs and product credibility.
- The research and development department worries about their credibility as perceived by senior management.
- The customer relations department worries about how to respond to retail and consumer questions and complaints.
- Your external relations committee worries about how to reinstate customer satisfaction without breaking the bank.
- Your customers worry about whether or not they should try your brand again.

STEP 3: DESIGN THE STRATEGY

Many companies face product recalls. To be on the safe side, these companies—to appease consumers—apologize first and take care of the problem later. From the consumers' point of view, this means removing the problem or danger from our sight, and then investigating to determine root causes.

Safeway Inc., a large chain of supermarkets, recalled its brand of taco shells because of claims that some shells contained genetically modified corn (thus far approved for animal consumption but not human consumption). According to the *The Wall Street Journal* (October 12, 2000), "In addition to Safeway's house brand of taco shells, the supermarket chain said it also is removing Mission Foods' own brand of taco shells from Safeway shelves." The products were pulled before the anti-biotechnology group's charges were investigated. The spokesperson for Safeway, Debra Lambert, was quoted as saying, "We're doing this out of an abundance of caution."

In the same month, Kellogg Co. closed several cereal manufacturing production lines while a supplier temporarily halted corn delivery to determine whether genetically modified grain got through the system and into Kellogg's production line (*The Wall Street Journal*, October 23, 2000). Even though Kellogg assured the public that, in all probability, no genetically altered grain found its way into Kellogg products, the production halt was labeled by spokesperson Chris Ervin as "purely precautionary."

This strategy brings new meaning to the old saying, "Shoot first and ask questions later." Protection of consumers' welfare, and of the company's reputation and credibility, come first. If no real problems are found, well, that's the price of doing business these days.

Now turn back to the case at hand. A sample solution for this case would include at least the following items.

Recall Strategy for the Case

1. Conduct a brainstorm with representatives of all relevant internal departments to identify:
   - Key stakeholders and the central message(s) they need to hear
   - Recall rollout procedures and timeline
   - Consistent statement about how the problem will be rectified
   - Explanation of how to return and exchange the watch for a new product or for return of purchase price

- Alternative options (e.g., rebate offer if another watch of your company's brand is purchased)

2. Document the key message(s) and recall action steps in a concise matrix for all relevant internal departments; ask for feedback and edit if necessary.
3. Gain approval for key message(s) and recall action steps from senior management.
4. Prepare and disseminate necessary peripherals (e.g., mailers, e-mail messages, news releases).

Methods and Media for the Case

Select methods and media such as:

- Announce recall to customers via regional sports magazines, newsletters, and announcements of upcoming sports events.
- Explain need for recall and procedures to follow to retailers via e-mail, fliers, telephone calls, and delivery packages of new product orders.
- Disseminate recall information to general consumer population via news releases to the media.

Internal Procedures for the Case

Proactively prepare internal personnel to handle the recall volume:

- Inform relevant customer interface people (e.g., receptionists) about the recall and tell them to refer all calls to the customer relations department.
- Prepare a script for your customer relations department to handle incoming consumer complaints and questions (via e-mail and telephone).
- Train customer relations department managers on procedures and scripts (train the trainer). Ensure that customers hear the following key messages: "We're sorry for the inconvenience," "Let me explain our simple recall procedures to fix this problem for you," and "We want to keep your business; we value you as a customer."
- Ask customer relations department managers to train their representatives on procedures and scripts.

Case 6-5   The Press Release

(Case purpose: Write a press release when a service breakdown occurs.)

STEP 1: REVIEW THE BIG PICTURE

You have some freedom of selection in this case. You may select any industry and company in which to work as the vice president of communications. Identify a service breakdown (e.g., slow airline flights, software application problems, poor customer service during merchandise returns) that results in many complaints.

Your task is to:

1. Identify an industry and company of your choice.
2. Describe the service breakdown (in one paragraph).
3. Write a press release that clarifies the problem, apologizes for the inconvenience or potential danger to clients/consumers, and states how the problem will be rectified.
4. Ensure that your press release contains a positive central idea about your organization.

STEP 2: ANALYZE FACTS AND EMOTIONS (F&Es)

The facts are as you imagine them for the purposes of this case. The emotions, even though your case differs from those selected by other people, generally encompass at least the following:

- Clients/consumers are upset over the inconvenience and/or potential danger.
- They want to understand *what* is wrong, *where* the issues occurred or could occur, and *why* it happened.
- They need to know *how* you will fix the problem.
- They need to hear you clarify *when* you will solve the problem (in the immediate future if possible).
- They need to be reassured that the person quoted in the press release (the *who*) is high enough in the organization to follow through on the promises.

STEP 3: DESIGN THE STRATEGY

Your press releases will differ because of the varying contexts that each of you selects for this case. However, B. L. Ochman, publisher of the biweekly marketing tactics newsletter, *What's Next Online*, suggested several critical success factors of the modern press release. Her suggestions were cited in her article entitled *The "Death" of the Traditional Press Release*, published in the summer 2000 edition of *The Public Relations Strategist* (pp. 16 and 18).

The following suggestions were adapted from Ms. Ochman's article. An effective press release comprises:

- A headline that catches people's attention.
- No more than 200 words (note: a typical 8.5" X 11" sheet contains 250 words).
- No more than five paragraphs (with just a few sentences in each paragraph).
- Paragraph headings that reflect the who, what, where, when, and why of the news
- A contact name, phone, e-mail, and URL (to make it easy for reporters who want additional information).

Ms. Ochman recommends, among other sites, *Yahoo! News Alerts*, for examples of good, succinct news releases.

Case 6-6 Advertising Gone Awry

(Case purpose: Create a damage control strategy when an ad offends people.)

STEP 1: REVIEW THE BIG PICTURE

Assume that you just heard about an ad that features a running shoe marketed for sports enthusiasts. A portion of the ad copy allegedly reads, "Right about now you're probably asking yourself, 'How can a trail running shoe with an outer sole designed like a goat's hoof help me avoid compressing my spinal cord into a Slinky(tm) on the side of some unsuspecting conifer. Thereby rendering me a drooling, misshapen non-extreme-trail running husk of my former self. Forced to roam the earth in a motorized wheelchair with my name, embossed on one of those cute little license plates you get at carnivals or state fairs, fastened to the back?'" (See *The Wall Street Journal*, October 26, 2000).

Your task is to:

- Decide if the publication of this ad could really occur in the year 2000 or after.
- Discuss how the company should approach damage control if people with disabilities claim that the ad is inappropriate.

STEP 2: ANALYZE FACTS AND EMOTIONS (F&Es)

Perhaps the less said, the better.

1. Facts: People need shoes.
2. Emotions: A company does not have to hurt one segment of the population to sell to another.

STEP 3: DESIGN THE STRATEGY

Unfortunately, this did, in fact, happen (see *The Wall Street Journal*, October 26, 2000).
   Nike chose a swift and thorough damage control strategy; they:

1. Pulled the ad from all publications (except one issue of one magazine).
2. Issued a formal apology.
3. Noted positive information such as the fact that they employ "people with different abilities."

   The problem, however, did not stop there. The ad agency also issued a formal apology. At least one of the magazines also noted their regrets. The costs, to reputations and to the bottom lines of these organizations, cannot be calculated.
   The author informally polled MBA students in three classrooms with this question: "Will you continue to buy Nike products or would you stop buying Nike products be-

cause of this ad?" Students said that they would continue buying Nike products because the company promptly pulled the ad and because the issue did not pose a safety threat to consumers.

Case 6-7   Electronic Break-In
(Case purpose: Plan how to cover the necessary information during an interview.)

STEP 1: REVIEW THE BIG PICTURE

For this case, you are the official media spokesperson for an investment firm. Two days ago, a hacker(s) broke into your company's system and it seems that valuable information may have been stolen. In particular, you are concerned that client account numbers and related data were taken. You contacted the Federal Bureau of Investigation to help you investigate the problem.

A journalist from *The Wall Street Journal* contacted you for an interview. Your task, before you speak with her, is to create an outline of the salient points you wish to communicate. For example, you'd want the public to know about the strict security standards used to date and the steps you will take to secure the accounts of your clients.

STEP 2: ANALYZE FACTS AND EMOTIONS (F&Es)

Facts

- Your system has been breached.
- You are investigating the problem.
- You do not yet know the identity of the hacker(s).
- The media contacted you, so you cannot delay communicating a message to the public.
- When this goes public, you will be inundated with calls from worried clients.

Emotions

- You are worried and your colleagues are worried.
- Your clients are worried.
- Potential clients may be afraid to open accounts with you.
- People will need reassurance that their current and/or new accounts will be safe.
- You want to portray an image that says to other potential hackers: "This only happened once and we are so on top of it that it won't happen again."

STEP 3: DESIGN THE STRATEGY

Microsoft experienced a hacker break-in during October 2000. A Microsoft spokes-person, in an October 27 *Wall Street Journal* article, stated that "Microsoft is moving ag-gressively to isolate the problem and ensure the security of our internal network. We are confident that the integrity of Microsoft source code remains secure." In an Octo-ber 30 *Wall Street Journal* article, a spokesperson stated that "We were aware of it im-mediately when it began. We tracked it in real time, knew what the person was doing." Statements like these are designed to reassure the public.

Your strategy for this case should at least cover the following salient points:

- We are fully aware of the problem. If you can truthfully say that your organiza-tion tracked the break-in from the onset, then the public can worry less about sneak attacks.
- We are working with authorities. If you are working with the authorities like the FBI, then the public may feel more assured that everything is being done.
- We have secured client accounts. If you can provide any details to reassure the pub-lic that information about their private lives is not lost to hackers, that is definitely a message that people need to hear.
- Our current security measures were strong. If you can assure people that the cur-rent system was not below standard, then you have a greater chance of assuring them that any upgrades will be even better.
- We will secure our system for the future. If you clearly state that necessary changes will be made to your security system, then you are, in effect, ensuring people that this won't happen again.
- We do offer (insert a product or service here). If you can end on a positive note, then readers will at least remember something good about your company.

What, if anything, is missing from this response? What might you change?

Case 6-8   Responding to Negative Internet Talk

(Case purpose: Formulate a response to widespread chat found on Internet.)

STEP 1: REVIEW THE BIG PICTURE

In this case, you are the CEO of a multinational organization (please select an industry with which you are familiar). We'll simply call your company, for the purposes of this case, Large Corporation. You are scheduled to speak at a news conference, 2 hours from now, to announce a merger with one of your rival companies. We'll label the smaller, rival organization Small Company.

Your company is larger and older than the rival organization, and your leadership has been consistently touted as *traditional*. The company with which you are merging has been in business for only 12 years and has been run by people now in the thirty-something age range. The co-owners of the smaller company, a female and a male, are known in the press as *rule-breakers* and *trend-setters* within your industry. Your company has a proportionally lower percentage of diverse managers when compared with the smaller company.

Your public relations analyst just walked into your office with disturbing news: Her department's regular monitoring of chat rooms and bulletin boards revealed a flurry of negative comments and accusations about your company's policies and leadership. She steps to your computer, goes online, and shows you a sample of the most recent comments (see upcoming sample comments).

She says, "We have to put a different spin on our merger announcement this morning. Our central message of 'enhanced services to loyal customers' may not work as well as we thought it would. This stuff makes it sound like many of their customers will take their business elsewhere because of our merger. Look, let me show you just a few samples—there are hundreds out there!"

Sample Chat Room/Bulletin Board Comments

Sample 1: Once again, the big fish is eating the little fish. Small Company has sold out. Their values of innovative thinking and creative handling of the small- to mid-size customer will be swallowed by Large Corporation. I, for one, am out of here. I'm going elsewhere and giving my business to someone else. I suggest you do the same.

Sample 2: So much for diversity. The guys in suits just took over Small Company. Now we'll lose the special service touches that we've come to expect from Small Company. Large Corporation just doesn't get it. How can they? They've run that place like big business for 75 years and they have no idea what today's younger market wants. Pull your business now before they mess it up for you.

Sample 3: Notice: Large Corporation and Small Company will announce their merger today. News conference scheduled for 10:30 A.M. What does this mean for the customers of Small Company? Just a few of your problems will include:

- No customized service for current Small Company customers. Large Corporation will focus on the big clients.
- Higher rates. Large Corporation is known for setting the highest rates in the industry.
- No understanding of the smaller customers' needs. Large Corporation has no dollar reason to focus on the little guy.
- Environmental policies at Small Company will go out the window. Large Corporation doesn't even understand the meaning of green.

Buyer beware: This is one merger where the little person will definitely get hurt.

Sample 4: Small Company clients—watch out! I just received a phone call from my Small Company account executive and he told me that my business won't make the short list cut after the merger. Large Corporation plans to weed out all small volume customers and this means the majority of Small Company clients. Get out now and make it difficult for Large Corporation before they do the same to you. Small Company management has, in effect, walked away from us. So there's no need for loyalty from Small Company clients!

Sample 5: Large Corporation and Small Company stockholders, take notice! This merger spells trouble. Neither company is as solvent as they say they are. Get out of this market now before the sky falls in.

Your task is to decide whether to edit the key message in your news conference statement ("enhanced services to loyal customers"), given the context of the Internet information and gossip. (In reality, your committee might at least include the following people to represent the points of view of various stakeholders: the CEO of Large Corporation, the co-owners of Small Company, the public relations analyst of Large Corporation, and the director of marketing for one or both organizations.)

STEP 2: ANALYZE FACTS AND EMOTIONS (F&Es)

Facts

The facts are disturbing yet simple:

- You have less than 2 hours to script a new message.
- You miscalculated the customer response to this merger.
- A definite *us* versus *them* mind-set simmers among some of your customer population.
- If your public relations department found the negative comments, so will the media.

Emotions

You might guess that at least the following emotions could occur here:

- Large Corporation executives may wish to discount the negative opinions located on the Internet.
- Small Company leadership may feel dismayed and worry about how the public will perceive them if they start any new ventures in the future.
- Some people may feel that there is no time to re-craft the news conference message, and "better left alone" could be their argument.
- If Large Corporation continues to miscalculate public response, then who knows what damage could be done to the organization's image?

STEP 3: DESIGN THE STRATEGY

This problem, evidenced in the open and rapid exchange of true facts, negative opinions, and false accusations, has increased with the widespread use of the Internet. No company can avoid facing the facts: A company's reputation is at risk because of the people who choose to key into chat rooms and bulletin boards.

Carole M. Howard and Wilma K. Mathews, in their book *On Deadline: Managing Media Relations* (3rd edition), state the facts quite succinctly (p. 263): "The Internet has put a great deal of power and reach into the hands of individuals. Anyone with a grudge and a computer can spew out hostile messages." Smart people in viable companies accept this ugly truth and incorporate it into their ongoing media management and crisis management planning efforts.

Mr. Ken Fields, Senior Vice President at Fleishman Hillard in St. Louis, notes that this case is on target because "technology has increased the speed of information exchange and increased the geographic breadth of information." Consequently, companies must be "prepared to respond quickly and broadly, and assemble the facts." The company in this case has already suffered a misstep because the public relations experts should have been aware, before the day of the news conference, of the negative comments floating around the Internet.

Mr. Fields notes that "chat rooms are often reflective of general opinions. However, anonymity gives people license to deal in the scandalous in chat rooms. Must companies respond to red flags on the Internet? Generally not, if the allegations are not well founded. However, whenever an announcement is imminent, you must be aware of all criticisms that may take place (e.g., during a merger). You must anticipate every conceivable negative comment before you make the announcement."

First, you should probably keep your key message of "enhanced services to loyal customers": there is no need to change it. In fact, Ken Fields suggests that this key message "does have the ability to be adapted to any question. It is a strong message that you could use to address issues from the Internet."

Second, troubleshoot potential questions and make sure that your spokesperson's answers can be turned back to your key message. Mr. Fields notes, "The truth is, you have to be very prepared. If it can be thought of, it can be asked. You must be prepared in two ways: (1) your key spokesperson must have a thorough knowledge of the facts, and (2) your spokesperson must know why your story is compelling to the media and to the people for whom they write." For example, in this case, Mr. Fields notes that the key message of "enhanced services to loyal customers" could be the central repository for concepts like "economies of scale, greater resources, and a more efficient distribution system." Consider, for example, a reporter's tough question about the customers of Small Company getting lost in the merger. The spokesperson could speak from the customer's point of view and promise fair prices because of the economies of scale, faster service because of the greater resources, and quicker delivery because of the more efficient distribution system.

Third, focus on the customers' point of view. A definite us versus them mind-set seems to simmer in the Internet comments; yet, the key message of "enhanced services to loyal customers" could be used to minimize this concern. Ken Fields states, "Make sure that you communicate a compelling story for the smaller company's customers. Vocal or not, many customers may be worried. The spokesperson must emphasize a compelling set of facts. When a major announcement is about to be made, there are usually very good reasons for the benefit of the company and the customers." The message should be scripted to highlight, from the Small Company customers' point of view, "why this can benefit me." Mr. Fields emphasizes, "As with everything, maintain focus on customers' needs and concerns."

Fourth, make sure the spokesperson is capable of responding to tough questions and returning to the key message. The team, according to Mr. Fields, must "provide the spokesperson with specific facts to back up your key message. I often recommend to clients that they picture in their minds a specific person, outside of their industry, similar to the target audience of the company's intended message. I ask clients to have that person in mind when crafting messages. Would this message persuade that person? Would this message make them understand why we're taking these actions?"

In closing, Mr. Fields recommends that the team must "do what you can to use news conferences and interviews to deliver your message rather than simply responding to the media's specific questions. Have a clear idea of what you want to say and restate your key message while answering every question."

Case 6-9   Questions to Explore and Discuss (Using the Web)

(Case purpose: Explore a sampling of crisis management Web sites.)

CRISIS MANAGEMENT WEB SITES

Laurence Barton, author of *Crisis in Organizations II* (2001) lists many crisis web sites in the appendix of his book. To work through the following questions, search a few of these online sites and discuss what you find with classmates or colleagues. Two sites noted by Barton include the Oregon School Boards Association Crisis Management Resources Web site and Sandra K. Clawson Freeo's Crisis Communication Plan: A Blue Print for Crisis Communication Web site. The two Web addresses follow:

- www.osba.org/hotopics/crismgmt/crisres.htm
- www.niu.edu/newsplace/crisis.html

Sample solutions to these cases are not given in this casebook because the online sites evolve and because your experiences and discussions will influence what you feel comprises a satisfactory solution.

Questions to Explore and Discuss

1. We plan to have an on-site counselor at our plant in the event of a disaster. Is this enough? (Clue: Would all people want to access a counselor in what they perceive to be a relatively public location?)
2. Should we plan to educate our general employee population about how to interact with survivors of a trauma occurring on company grounds? (Clue: Would it help people to know *how* to speak with survivors: what to say, what not to say?)
3. Is it true that counseling and interventions offered through our company should stop within 5 working days after the trauma occurred? (Clue: Does severity impact transition time?)

4. Isn't it true that how my company responds to a crisis over the long-term is more important than how we respond the day of the trauma? (Clue: Think about on-the-spot news coverage that you may have witnessed on television.)

5. Where can I go to find sample crisis plans? (Clue: Review the sites previously mentioned and others originally cited in Laurence Barton's book.)

6. Once the crisis is over, can't we destroy all the documents that we generated? (Clue: For what reasons might you need the documents? Which office in your organization is best prepared to file these documents?)

7. Once the initial crisis event is past and we have thoroughly investigated the root cause, should we position the event, during news interviews, under a category? (Clue: Would you want to restate the numerous details each time or would you want to use a summary phrase to explain the issue?)

Bibliography

Barton, L. (2001). *Crisis in Organizations II*. Cincinnati: South-Western College Publishing. (This book lists crisis Web resources in the appendix.)

Bridis, T., and Buckman, R. (2000, October 27). Hackers break into Microsoft's network. *The Wall Street Journal*, A3, A8, (Gary Fields contributed to this article).

Bridis, T., Buckman, R., and Fields, G. (2000, October 30). Microsoft says firm detected hacker quickly. *The Wall Street Journal*, A3, A15.

Eig, J. (2000, October 23). Kellogg halts cereal lines for corn tests. *The Wall Street Journal*, A32.

Grimes, A. (2000, October 26). Nike rescinds ad, apologizes to disabled people. *The Wall Street Journal*, B20.

Howard, C. M., and Mathews, W. K. (2000). *On Deadline: Managing Media Relations* (3rd Ed.). Prospect Heights, Illinois: Waveland Press, Inc.

Jefferson County Public Schools. *Emergency Management Plan (EMP)*. Golden, Colorado 80401-0001.

Kilman, S., and Spurgeon, D. (2000, October 12). Safeway recalls its taco-shell brand on charge it contains unapproved corn. *The Wall Street Journal*, A8.

Ochman, B. L. (2000). The "Death" of the Traditional Press Release. *The Public Relations Strategist* 6, no. 2, 16, 18.

CHAPTER 7

Manager as Conflict Mediator

Conflict: A Constant Threat

Managers know that point in a meeting when discussions become difficult, when hope of a common direction is lost. Managers know that from this point forward communication becomes more labor-intensive, more tenuous. Good managers understand that the meaning of every word and the signals portrayed by body language have now escalated in importance.

Suzette Haden Elgin, in her book *The Gentle Art of Verbal Self-Defense for Business Success*, states that "Communication breakdowns at the executive/professional level almost always result from reality gaps—radical differences in the way people perceive situations" (p. 8). The truth of her statement is understatement at its best.

Point of view is critical in verbal dialogue; point of view is not just an issue in written communications. Each person must intently listen to others, correctly interpret what was said, and respond in a nonthreatening manner. This is no small task because it requires *understanding* other points of view. Every interaction is tinged by a person's perception of the world and of any given situation; this perception leads to that person's unique reaction.

Much of what we call perception and reaction is based on habitual behavior, learned behavior. Anne Fisher notes in her 1998 *Fortune* article entitled "Success Secret: A High Emotional IQ," that there are two ways to change mental habits: (1) "notice when you are falling into it," and (2) "practice a different response."

It is this author's belief that we, as managers, must separate *fact* from *emotion* (see Case 5-1 in Chapter 5) if we are to understand others' points of view and avoid marginally successful perceptions and reactions. If managers are to separate fact from emotion, then we must first control our own emotions. Robert K. Cooper and Ayman Sawaf, in *Executive EQ: Emotional Intelligence in Leadership and Organizations*, propose a three-step process for managing emotional energy (p. 35):

1. "Acknowledge and feel the emotion" (don't pretend emotions don't exist).
2. "Listen to the information or feedback the emotion is giving you . . . e.g., 'Which of my principles, values, or goals is at stake here?'"
3. "Guide . . . the emotional energy into an appropriate, constructive response."

It is this author's opinion that a well-prepared manager (one who mentally troubleshoots situations before they happen) does a better job of managing emotions, perceiving situations accurately, and responding professionally. The cases in this chapter cover difficult organizational ground. Review Tables 7-1 and 7-2 ("Coaching Techniques") to identify how to:

- Distribute time and energy in a meeting or coaching session when conflict is inherent.
- Prepare for and close a meeting where there is conflict.

TABLE 7-1   Coaching Techniques—Steps[a]

Step 1: Explain the What and Why (20%)	Step 2: Explain the Big Picture and Ask the Employee to Outline a Hypothetical Approach (50%)	Step 3: Coach the Details (30%)
State purpose and importance of desired outcomes.	• Ask how and why questions. • Actively listen. • Probe and clarify. • Focus eye contact and body direction. • Avoid showing judgment; delay negative emotions of dismay or anger. • Use the *five why* technique (ask why until you reach the source problem). • Paraphrase to identify person's values and assumptions (feelings and memories).	• State what is correct. • Explain what was missed and how to change or improve. • State benefits.

[a]Column width relates to proportional time spent on each step during interaction.

TABLE 7-2   Coaching Techniques—Tips

Before the Session:	*During the Session:*	*At the Conclusion of the Session:*
Sketch a **visual** to illustrate the issue and a possible solution.	Sketch the visual after the conversation is well under way. The person must feel that his/her perspectives are reflected.	Refer to the visual while agreeing on next steps.
Identify the **behaviors** at issue. A drop file (dated notes on what the person says and does) will help.	State examples of what the person says and does; avoid statements like "your attitude . . ." Assumptions about attitudes can be incorrect and escalate problems.	Restate a few key behaviors to change or improve.
Review the behaviors and identify **trends.**	Listen to one or two answers and say, "I do understand what you are saying." Then state the trends demonstrated by what the person says and does. This avoids the *he said, she said* syndrome about individual situations. Noting the *who, what, when, where,* and *how* (without assuming the *why*) can help prove trends.	Restate how changing/ improving a few key behaviors will reduce or eliminate the trends.
Focus on **current** versus **desired/required** results — and the **choices** the person can make.	Clearly state what occurs now and what needs to occur. People respond better to language focused on *results* (not *consequences*).	Note your belief that the person will make the right choices.
List a few **probing techniques** that you can glance at during the session if and when emotions heat up.	Get the person to think out loud: • "I'm not clear on details. Tell me more." • "What do you value about your work?" • "Why did that happen?" (Answer.) "Why do you think that occurred?" (Do this until you identify the root causes under the symptoms).	Summarize that everyone can maximize results by minimizing negative emotions. Set a follow-up session and, if appropriate, develop a documented action plan (to be signed by relevant parties).

Use four steps to approach and role-play the cases:

1. Organize into small teams and read a case.
2. Select members from *different* teams to role-play the manager and the problem person. As a team, plan the manager's approach and the problem person's negative behaviors. Don't explain your approaches to opposing teams before the role-play.

3. Conduct the role-play.
4. Debrief the role-play: Identify critical manager approaches and problem person behaviors. Discuss what worked and what didn't—from both points of view. Discuss alternative strategies for handling the difficult situation. The value of these cases derives from the rich discussion, as well as the disagreements, among class members.

CASES

Case 7-1   The Sneaker

(Case purpose: Coach a difficult employee.)

STEP 1: REVIEW THE BIG PICTURE

You manage a department of 10 people: nine professionals (all with *manager* in their job titles) and one clerical support person. Performance reviews were completed 2 months ago; the clerical person (CP) received competent ratings (the average of all managers' ratings). Recently, however, CP's behavior radically changed.

- **2 weeks ago.** Manager A asked CP to type an external client proposal that morning. Manager A returned from a meeting at noon to discover the document not completed. When questioned by Manager A, CP responded: "I didn't have time." Manager A asked you, as vice president of the entire group, to intervene. When you questioned CP, CP replied, "I was swamped. I didn't have time."
- **1 week ago.** Manager E asked CP to make 20 photocopies of a 10-page document and staple them. CP returned the copies, but they were not stapled. Manager E did it himself, but asked you if something is up with CP.
- **Today.** You asked CP to attend and take notes at a 2-hour briefing session (from 10:00 A.M. to noon) with a client. You asked CP to attend the 2-hour session and then take the regular hour-long lunch. Another manager needed CP to finalize some PowerPoint cells for an international presentation (the manager flies out today). You haven't seen CP and it is now 2:30 P.M.

The following facts complicate this case: The previous manager of your department did not complete thorough or accurate performance reviews of CP. Your managers tell you that, until you began managing the department 6 months ago, they'd never seen copies of CP's formal, written performance evaluations. When you shared these previous copies, a quotable quote from one of the managers was, "CP was never as competent as these previous evaluations. I know CP's performance was pretty good for a while when you took over, but now CP's back to previous behavior."

The actual conversation between you and CP, upon CP's return at 2:35 P.M. is found in Box 7-1.

STEP 2: ANALYZE FACTS AND EMOTIONS (F&Es)

At this point, CP's manager might say, "Oh no!" Why? First, an experienced manager knows that CP's behavior is just the tip of the iceberg. Second, a seasoned manager knows that CP's behavior, if not remedied immediately, will continue. (Pareto's Law might be applied here: 80 percent of a manager's time is easily spent on the 20 percent of the people who demonstrate problems.) Third, a manager surveying the long-term picture (i.e., before and during this manager's tenure) would understand that managerial action is somewhat limited by the solid written performance evaluations of the previous manager.

BOX 7-1

Manager's Conversation with CP

YOU: CP, where have you been? The 2-hour session ended at noon.

CP: I went to lunch and then I stepped upstairs for Gloria's going away party. It was actually informative! I learned so much that is new around here!

YOU: CP, I asked you to attend the 2-hour session and then to go to lunch. I don't understand.

CP: Oh! But I didn't intend to go.

YOU: But you did go. And, you did not call to let us know where you were. Manager A needed those PowerPoint cells before she left town.

CP: If I had intended to go, I would have called you.

We want to look at *how* CP responded to you, the manager. But let's first do a reality check. A reasonable definition of a *reasonable employee* says that this employee:

- Does not disappear when others require deliverables or services.
- Does fulfill job duties, when possible, in a timely fashion.
- Does not avoid true issues by inventing ridiculous sidetracks.
- Does attempt, painful though it may be, to settle differences of opinion.

You must understand, from the onset, that CP is not manipulating the *facts*. Instead, CP is going for the sneak attack: CP throws your factual logic out the window by focusing on the *emotional* point: "But I didn't intend to go." CP is not behaving like a reasonable employee.

CP could hope that you grow increasingly befuddled by CP's approach and simply halt your offense. And, yes, some managers do stop here. Yet, these same managers never settle the *root cause* of the problem; instead, they continue to deal with the *symptoms* week after week.

STEP 3: DESIGN THE STRATEGY

Forget the Facts for a While; Focus on Emotions First

Don't continue to ask CP, "Why?" Trust me. You won't get a logical answer (at least not an answer that you consider logical). Deal with CP on CP's current level: *emotions*.

Shift gears entirely. Ask CP which tasks have been most *enjoyable* in the job (long-term and in recent weeks). Ask CP which tasks create the greatest *feelings* of accomplishment. Ask and then listen, listen, listen. When CP stops talking, ask a few probing questions, but stick to *emotion* questions from CP's point of view. In other words, don't ask CP *why* CP's behavior exists; instead ask CP about the *what, when, and where of*

CP's feelings. If you ask CP a *why* question at this stage of the game, you only put CP on the defensive. Instead, ask *what* CP likes best; ask *when* CP does these tasks, and ask *where* CP usually completes these tasks; you'll identify valuable information about CP's preferences (The World According to CP).

It will come as no surprise that CP thinks and feels quite differently than you. You will, however, arm yourself with knowledge about how CP *thinks and feels* and, therefore, *why* CP disappeared on a tour in the middle of a perfectly good workday. You won't like the answer; but you'll have an answer that you couldn't get by verbally cornering CP.

You may discover that CP likes being around people; CP excels at it, in fact. Everyone enjoys CP's personality. However, CP may not consistently balance the *push* of tedious tasks against the *pull* of interesting people and activities. CP chose with *emotions* (i.e., this *feels* like fun) as opposed to *facts* (i.e., I *need* to get back to my desk).

You, as manager, have your work cut out for you in coaching CP. You must:

1. Ask probing questions (first focus on *what, when, where*; later focus on *how* and *why* questions).
2. Sketch a picture (as CP talks) of what current state versus desired state looks like. You want CP to believe that what CP says, and feels, somehow relates to the sketched solution. Focus on what CP must *say* and *do* to achieve success, don't focus on CP's alleged attitudes. (See Chapter 5 for ideas on translating words into pictures).
3. Get CP to restate, in one or two sentences, what CP must say and do from now on (to keep this particular issue from recurring and to achieve success).
4. Focus first on CP's emotions, and then focus on the facts (i.e., CP's behavioral trends and steps toward improvement). If CP believes you've understood CP's feelings, then you have a better chance of helping CP change specific work behaviors.

Remember Suzette Haden Elgin's words (*The Gentle Art of Verbal Self-Defense for Business Success*): "Communication breakdowns ... almost always result from reality gaps—radical differences in the way people perceive situations."

Good luck! In some cases, the bottom line may be that CP is better suited to a different job: Perhaps a job with more autonomy and room for interpersonal interaction.

Test Your Managerial Strategy

Test your ability to strategize difficult coaching meetings: Read the following solution scenarios related to Case 7-1 and identify what might cause problems with each scenario. Assume that a manager just called CP into the office to determine why CP disappeared from work duties for several hours today.

Strategy 1: "CP, I'm extremely displeased with you. I specifically told you to go to the meeting, go to lunch, and then return to work. I cannot imagine why you did not listen to me."

Problems with Strategy 1: This manager, unfortunately, is controlled by her own emotions. Her choice of words shows CP that the manager is more concerned about being disobeyed than about CP's job performance. CP could easily respond, in kind, from an emotional viewpoint and then the two people are locked in a battle of wills.

Strategy 2: "CP, I've been so worried about you. Are you okay? I'm just glad that you are okay. I thought perhaps you'd had an accident."

Problems with Strategy 2: This manager demonstrates an overly protective stance. If CP so chooses, this manager can easily be manipulated. This manager has communicated that any excuse will be perceived as acceptable, since CP is "safe."

Strategy 3: "CP, sit down. We need to talk. Your work performance, until recently, has been acceptable. Now, however, we are experiencing problems with your behavior. If this keeps up, I want you to know that I may have to look into removing you from this position."

Problem with Strategy 3: This manager rapidly escalates the conversation to threat of a job loss for CP. This leaves CP little room for a calm discussion. CP must now focus on saving a job in jeopardy instead of responding to the issue at hand: why CP did not return to work on time.

A Final Note

Managers may find that some of their most difficult communications fall within the realm of employee performance conversations. Consider conceptualizing your strategy for these conversations along a continuum (shown later in this section).

Managers need to see options for handling these difficult situations with employees. Managers who see options (i.e., choices) are better prepared to appropriately strategize performance conversations and manage their own emotions during such conversations. As the oft-repeated saying goes, "There should be no surprises in a performance review." Managers are obligated to first coach (repeating this step if necessary) their employees. If managers are sure that the employees know how to perform the task, then they can proceed into the coaching and reprimand mode, if and when necessary.

Any moves toward warnings and actions to terminate should be purposeful, fair, and thoroughly documented: The last step in the continuum should never be taken lightly. (Of course, in the event of behaviors that threaten the safety or lives of others, the act to terminate should be handled according to appropriate legal steps.)

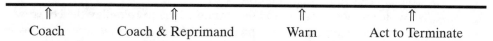

⇑	⇑	⇑	⇑
Coach	Coach & Reprimand	Warn	Act to Terminate

A manager's fair and factual reaction to an employee's behavior should always override any personal, emotional reaction. A fair manager moves along the continuum from left (coach) to the right.

Case 7-2 Political Waters!
(Case purpose: Navigate the situation when a peer tries to damage your reputation.)

STEP 1: REVIEW THE BIG PICTURE

Assume that you are a senior level manager in an international corporation. The organization is in a period of great transition: You've seen downsizing, reengineering, and closing field offices during the last few months. The executive team is comprised of six executives (gender is mixed). You are part of the senior management team reporting to one of the executive team members.

Another senior level manager—with your same "director" job title, but managing a different group—is known for spreading gossip. This other director tells some executive team members that *you* say negative things to your people about the strategic direction of the corporation.

The director also told executive team members the same kinds of stories about at least two of your colleagues in the corporation. You know, however, that these colleagues are positive people who are team players. (For the record, you are also a team player and you have not presented negativity in front of your employees.) One executive, a personal friend of yours, told you this sordid story last week at lunch.

As a team (three to five people):

1. Discuss the *possible political ramifications* of *ignoring this situation* versus *dealing with* it in a proactive way. Talk about how you—given your culture and background—feel about this situation.
2. Select team members from two separate teams to role-play the conversation between you (the first director) and the other director who is spreading gossip.

STEP 2: ANALYZE FACTS AND EMOTIONS (F&Es)

Have you found yourself in the middle of a political situation similar to this one? If you've worked any length of time in any organization, the answer is probably yes. Let's cut to the bottom line on this case: The issue—at least the issue that you can control—is not one of fair play. The issue is how you will handle the situation.

The other director, the one spreading gossip, does not operate under your rules of fair play (fairly obvious, isn't it?). So (using *if, then* contingency planning), if your fair play rules differ so drastically, then you have little chance of changing the other director's attitude and behavior. The other director, for reasons well beyond your understanding or control, *perceives* the world as a place where only a few can win. The other director's *point of view* forces challenges between peers instead of collaborative efforts. The other director views his or her *positioning* with executive management as a *win/lose proposition against you*. And, this director intends to win by making the competition look bad.

So, what are your chances (i.e., *options*)? You could:

1. Ignore the situation.
2. Speak privately to your colleagues.
3. Copy, as appropriate, the executives on some of your positive memos and departmental communications.
4. Speak privately to other members of the executive team.
5. Confront the director.
6. Do all of these.

Let's use *if, then contingency planning* (in ascending order of risk) to think through the best strategy (see Table 7-3). Consider whether you are prepared to live with the consequences of any given *then* scenario.

STEP 3: DESIGN THE STRATEGY

If you're smart and cautious, you'll follow a sequence of steps similar to the escalating steps in the previous table. Whatever you do, you must first analyze the organizational context, the power structure, the political risks, and your ability to survive or leave if the

---

TABLE 7-3   If, Then Contingency Planning

If you . . .	Then:
Ignore the situation	• The other director continually spreads false gossip. • Your credibility may diminish.
Speak privately to your colleagues	• You check for more facts first before doing anything (fact finding is a good thing, but remember that strong emotions color facts). • Trust colleagues to maintain confidentiality about your conversation (always a risk).
Copy, as appropriate, the executives on some of your positive memos and departmental communications	• You informally (and in an indirect way) keep the executives apprised of the *good* messages you share with your department and others in the organization. • You may buy some positive press without ever telling on the competitive director.
Speak privately to other members of the executive team	• You may garner empathy if executive team members also witness the bad side of the other director (you cannot be sure; this is risky). • You lose credibility if executive team members have not witnessed the bad side of the other director (e.g., you may find yourself buried under the epitaph: "It was just a personality clash.").
Confront the director	• You run the risk of appearing overly emotional. • You look foolish if the director denies the situation. • The director will probably ask, "Who told you this?" • You put the director on notice that you know the real score. Sometimes, this is all you can do. But at least the other director knows you aren't oblivious.
Do all of these	• You follow a basic rule for survival in political waters: Escalate slowly, with caution, and with sufficient facts. Prepare to handle *any* consequence.

issues escalate negatively. With any luck, you may not complete every painful step in the escalation process. With luck, the other director will make a career-limiting move or career-terminating move (also known among some firms as a CLM or CTM), or the other director will leave the organization. Or you might leave the organization for a better job.

Chances are, however, that the other director will stay put for the near future. Why? This type of personality needs to control the immediate environment out of *insecurity*; they rarely prepare (i.e., change) for new challenges in unknown environments.

Teams responding to this case need to understand that sometimes just letting the rumor-spreading director "know that you know" is all that you can control. Role-playing students must not feel as though they lost if they cannot convince the gossiping director to change his or her ways.

Case 7-3   Where's the Secondary Research?

(Case purpose: Manage a group of unwilling cross-functional team members.)

STEP 1: REVIEW THE BIG PICTURE

Assume that you are a middle level manager in a large company (e.g., director level). You've been named the lead manager on an external client project; your consulting team is comprised of seven cross-functional members (all employed within your company) as follows:

- One (1) team lead/project manager (i.e., you).
- Two (2) research managers from your company's Research Department.
- Two (2) systems analysts from your company's Information Department.
- One (1) communications manager from your company's Creative Department.
- One (1) programmer from your company's Client Intranet Development Group.

You just returned from your client's world headquarters; your team met with people representing several departments and functions within the client's organization. Your key client sent 22 documents home with you! The documents include nine (9) primary research reports detailing your client's business within the context of their industry. (For the purposes of this case, you won't review all these reports!)

Your team must get a handle (i.e., analyze and understand) on these data. Your team must compare the primary research data against the qualitative information learned while on site with the client. Then, and only then, can your team proceed with a preliminary plan for the client.

You asked the two research managers to conduct secondary research on the nine primary research reports and present a summary to your team. You asked that their summary be ready for yesterday's 3:00 P.M. meeting. Yesterday's meeting ran long, and you did not get to their summary. However, you learned during a coffee break yesterday that the research managers had not completed the secondary research. In fact, they told you that they would *not* complete the task!

Now (today), you are in a dilemma. You must have the secondary research summary in 3 days. You do not have time to complete the work yourself, and other team members are not qualified to do so. The research managers do not report directly to you; they are on this cross-functional team for the purposes of this client project.

As a small team (three to five people):

- *Discuss* how you will handle this situation. Whom will you contact, how, and when? What will you say to them? How far will you escalate this issue (e.g., will you tell the research managers' director now or wait until you speak with the research managers)?
- *Role-play* your conversation (as team lead/project manager) with the research managers. The role-play works best if a person from one team role-plays the team lead/project manager and two people from a second team role-play the two research managers.
- You may also decide to role-play a conversation with the research managers' director.

You will have more than two people in this role-play (one team lead/project manager and two research managers).

STEP 2: ANALYZE FACTS AND EMOTIONS (F&Es)

Let's use the familiar SWOT analysis (Strengths, Weaknesses, Opportunities, and Threats), *with a twist*. Instead of analyzing industry, market, or organizational factors, let's analyze the *personalities* and *competencies* (i.e., knowledge, attitudes, skills, and habits) of the key players on your team.

For our purposes in this case, we'll focus on you, the two research managers, and the research managers' director, and we'll apply the following definitions to SWOT (see Table 7-4):

- Strengths: Competencies or personality traits you know to be true.
- Weaknesses: Missing competencies or personality issues you know to be true.
- Opportunities: Unknown information (i.e., questions you should ask).
- Threats: Things that could happen (i.e., prepare yourself for these *if, then contingencies*).

What are the benefits of modifying the SWOT analysis? Several; you will:

1. Identify the balance (or imbalance!) between the *facts* (competencies) and *emotions* (personalities).
2. Avoid unfounded assumptions by identifying only *known* strengths and weaknesses.
3. Identify relevant probing questions *before* you find yourself in the middle of an uncomfortable conversation about performance issues.
4. Spend less time arguing over what are only *symptoms* of the problem.

TABLE 7-4 SWOT Analysis

Key Player	Strengths (known to be true)	Weaknesses (known to be true)	Opportunities (unknown / ask questions)	Threats (if, then / prepare yourself)
Team lead / project manager (you)	(List your own here.)	(List your own here.)	Do you avoid confrontation? Do you attack rather than fact-find? Do you solve the short-term problem and the long-term root cause(s)?	If you complete secondary research yourself (to avoid conflict), then will a poor precedent be set? If you outsource the secondary research, then will quality be assured?
Two research managers	Employed as qualified research managers.	Didn't inform you of incomplete work/deadline problem. Say they will not complete research; do not provide alternative solutions.	Influenced by conflicting project demands? Unwilling to perform secondary research (preference for primary research)?	If you force a discussion with research managers, then will interpersonal issues escalate? If you talk to research managers at same time, then will you get the whole story?
Director of two research managers	Unknown	Unknown	Will the director support project needs or research managers (in spite of who is right)? Can the director assign additional resources? Will the director admit (manager to manager) if these issues have arisen before?	If you escalate problem to director, then will research managers resent or mistrust you? If you escalate problem to director and she or he doesn't support project needs, then will you lose credibility with team?

5. Be more likely to uncover the *root causes* of the problem.
6. Present a stronger *image* in the discussions about the problem.

STEP 3: DESIGN THE STRATEGY

1. Consider how the key players might complete their separate SWOT analyses. If you think from other persons' points of view, then you have a better chance of creating a SWOT analysis that can be successfully applied to solving the problem.

2. It can also be helpful to pair members of different teams together for a role-play (before a real problem occurs!):
   - One member of a team could role-play the team lead/project manager.
   - Two members of another team could role-play the research managers.
3. Ask remaining members to debrief the role-play (e.g., were the right probing questions asked, did the team lead/project manager maintain control of the meeting, was the root cause identified?).
4. Ask respective teams to outline how they approached their SWOT analysis.
5. Discuss how *assumptions* made during the SWOT analysis affect the *outcomes* of the problem-solving attempts. Remember that assumptions help define behavior (whether or not we recognize this fact at the time).

Case 7-4   Communication Plan (Internal Focus)

(Case purpose: Create a communication plan to deliver bad news.)

STEP 1: REVIEW THE BIG PICTURE

This case focuses on an organization in trouble: This company must reduce product lines, close plants, and lay off people. If this organization does not effectively handle internal and external communications, then managers are faced with unnecessary conflict and mistrust. See Case 6-1 ["Communication Plan (Media Focus)"] in Chapter 6, for how to handle the media.

Background

Alpha Beta (AB) Computers is a hardware/software company in operation for approximately 13 years and with 18 product lines. AB's world headquarters are in Chicago; 120 managers and 1,280 employees are distributed among the executive, design, sales, and marketing divisions. There are 10 manufacturing and distribution points in the United States: three in the eastern region (total employee population is 750), one in the Midwestern region (population is 250), two in the southern region (population is 527), and four in the western region (population is 1,710).

Current Status

The distribution chain includes value-added resellers (VARs, with 95 percent of the business) and AB-only retail (comprising 5 percent of the business). The sales managers ($n = 2,000$) and sales representatives ($n =$ approximately 17,000; in constant turnover) are the target audiences for the product knowledge and sales incentives programs driven down by corporate. Two computer companies are rapidly encroaching on the market share and AB's profits have dropped by 12 percent in the last quarter. Overall profitability and sales volume trends are also on a downswing.

Wave One of the President's Strategy

The company president decided that consolidating from 18 to 12 product lines is the first wave of attack against the issues facing the company. The hardware lines won't change; however, revamped software lines will eliminate redundancies and slow features (as identified through customer satisfaction data). Any software with a poor sales performance record is in jeopardy.

Wave Two of the President's Strategy

The company president made a difficult decision to downsize within the next 6 months (less time is better). The downsizing will be positioned as the second wave of attack against the company's problems. One manufacturing and distribution point in the east and one in the south will close. Head count will drop by 350 in the east (because of the Long Island closing) and by 275 in the south (the Atlanta site is closing). Remaining sites in the east and south will pick up the slack (i.e., take over the work).

Overview of Two Assignments

Assume that you are the consulting team assigned to AB Computers; AB asked you to complete two assignments:

1. **Speech.** Write a *speech* for the president to deliver to the entire organization.
2. **Work Plan.** Create a *high-level work plan* that organizes all events surrounding the plant closings, downsizing, and product consolidations.

Assignment 1: Speech

Write a speech for the company president to deliver via simultaneous videoconference and on-site headquarters meeting. The purpose of the speech is to *set the stage* for upcoming changes and to get people *on board*.

Rumors spread across the company regarding the plant closings and product changes. Limit the speech to 2 minutes: This equates to two double-spaced pages of approximately 250 words each.

Before beginning, review two relevant sections related to speech writing in Chapter 1, "Manager as Communication Coach" ("Example: Look for Analogies and Metaphors in Speeches," and "Edit a Rough Draft to Include More Visual Images"). Write a first draft and share it with your team members. Then, edit the speech and write a second draft. Give the second draft to the instructor.

Assignment 2: Work Plan

You must think through the *who, what, when, where, why*, and *how* of the critical events surrounding the downsizing and product consolidations. The purpose of creating such a work plan is to ensure that:

- The sequence of events makes logical sense (i.e., executives, plant managers, and supervisors are saying the same things and following one consistent plan).

- The right people hear the right messages at the right times (e.g., a critical client does-n't want to hear about AB's changes from a supplier; AB must deliver the message).
- All stakeholders' perspectives and needs are considered.

This exercise is difficult to complete alone and it is also difficult to complete by committee. The most efficient approach to this exercise is to adapt the *affinity diagram* method to this task. As a team, for example, follow these steps:

1. Brainstorm a list of the key stakeholders (e.g., employees at headquarters, employ-ees at plants to be closed, supervisors, managers, executives, board members, stock-holders, suppliers, retail personnel, families, communities where plants are to be closed, media, etc.).
2. Ask each consulting team member to focus on one or more of the key stakeholder groups. Each team member silently thinks about what the group(s) will need to know and writes one key event on a self-stick note (one event per note). Each note should begin with a verb and should be no more than 12 words in length. Examples:
   - Distribute press releases to media (as president finishes corporate-wide speech).
   - Hire outplacement firm.
   - Prepare "What to Say When" package for managers and supervisors (e.g., answers to frequently asked questions).
   - Hire additional security prior to day when people are laid off.
3. Place all self-stick notes on a wall, and as a team, rearrange them until the sequence makes sense. Then look for events and/or stakeholders that have been overlooked; add self-stick notes as necessary.
4. On a flip chart sheet, draw two columns headed "Key Events" and "Timing." Arrange the self-stick notes under Key Events and list the sequential timing for each key event under Timing, by week.
5. Arrange all the self-stick notes, in sequential order, on as many flip chart sheets as needed.
6. Then, given the 6-month time frame noted for this case, write a logical timing for each event. The easiest way to do this (for the purposes of this high-level work plan) is to assign each key event a week number; for example: week 1, week 2, week 12. Obviously, several key events may occur simultaneously and thus have the same week number listed.

This forms the basis of your high-level work plan; future tasks (*not* included in this case) would include writing all the necessary communication documents, keeping man-agers and supervisors informed of what to say when, etc.

STEP 2: ANALYZE FACTS AND EMOTIONS (F&Es)

Let's analyze the facts and emotions for Case 6-1 and the key factors involved in the two assignments (see Table 7-5):

1. Speech
2. High-level Work Plan

TABLE 7-5   Facts and Emotions

Facts (Overview)	Emotions (Preliminary List)
• AB Computer's status against the competition is dwindling.	• This relatively young company, and its people, will suffer because of these tough decisions.
• AB Computer customers, through satisfaction surveys, have identified issues with certain software packages.	• People will listen with their emotions during the president's speech (e.g., I have two kids in college, I hope I'm not laid off; our executive team won't suffer, us little guys do all the hurting; I hope Mary gets laid off, I consistently do more work than she does).
• Competitive companies' products are purchased and valued by customers.	
• The president's (with the implied backing of the board and executive team) decision to consolidate product lines, close two plants, and lay off personnel is definite.	• If the wrong information leaks out in an unorganized fashion, the credibility of the company and its management will suffer.
	• If the media gets hold of this news before management is ready to release it, we will look bad (see Chapter 6).

Sample solutions for the three assignments follow. No sample solution is perfect. Review the samples as starting points for your discussions; share your experiences, and blend ideas and perspectives.

STEP 3: DESIGN THE STRATEGY

Assignment 1: Speech—Sample Solution

The speech draft in Table 7-6 contains critical elements for this situation. The left column tells you *why* a portion of the speech is important; the right column contains *key excerpts* of the speech (a few phrases were edited: those appear in brackets).

Discuss this first draft. What are the strengths and weaknesses? What would you write differently? What would you add or delete?

Assignment 2: High-Level Work Plan—Sample Solution

Table 7-7 represents a *first and partial draft* of the critical steps inherent in a corporate-wide communications work plan. A cross-functional team of middle- to senior-level managers would create such a work plan (senior executives simply don't have the time during a crisis event). Then, the first draft would be amended, edited, and sequenced to fit the context of the organization, the culture, and the situation. The cross-functional middle- and senior-management team would work closely with executives to ensure that the right messages are communicated, in the right way, at the right times.

Any unforeseen event, such as the media learning of the downsizing before the company's formally scheduled announcement, would result in revisions to such a work plan.

There is no single best solution to the work plan. Capitalize on the expertise of team members who have experienced such situations and discuss the pros and cons of implementing key events at certain times. In reality, this work plan is a living document that will undergo constant revision.

TABLE 7-6 Speech Draft

President's Speech (First Draft)	*Why This Is Important*
Good morning. First, I acknowledge those of you in our headquarters auditorium as well as our plant and field office people joining in through videoconference. I thank all of you for leaving your work to attend this critical meeting.	Listeners know that headquarters, plant, and field office people all hear the speech at the same time. This eliminates some nonproductive time after the speech when people call coworkers in other locations to say, "Have you heard . . . ?"
As you know, we are in the midst of difficult times. Our competition has increasingly eroded our market share. Our customers have shared some dissatisfaction with some of our hardware and software lines. AB Computers is 13 years old; some of you have been with us from the beginning. You've seen us evolve; you've seen us change before in response to our customers' needs.	
And now, we find ourselves needing to change again. Yes, *it is time for change*.	The president must acknowledge the difficult times yet focus on the positive.
	Since so many people tune in and out of a bad news speech, a simple central idea that gets repeated often is necessary: It is time for change.
You know the facts; you've heard them repeatedly during the last few months. But allow me to repeat them again. Our profits have dropped by 12 percent in the last quarter alone. Our profitability and sales volume have been on downward trends for the last several quarters. And, as you know, two of our competitors' computers have particularly challenged our hardware line. These continuing facts leave us with one overarching conclusion: *it is time for change.*	Listeners need to be reminded of the facts since they have emotional responses to this speech (and the situation).
	The president needs to reiterate the facts before the tough announcements.
I have led an executive team during recent months to analyze these issues. We have looked at our situation from every imaginable angle. We have reduced our discretionary budgets and taken other measures to cut back costs. But our problems have continued and we now face a critical point. *It is time for change.*	People need to hear their leader take some measure of responsibility.
While my next statements are quite difficult for me, I take responsibility for making these final decisions. You've all heard the rumors in recent months. The wildest rumor I've heard is that AB Computers will shut down. Let me assure you that this is not the case.	People also need to know that the president is aware of the ever-escalating rumor mill (always inherent in these situations).
We must change just enough about our business, however, to remain competitive and eventually climb the path toward success again. Our next steps include two critical strategies:	The president must state the next steps succinctly, yet show an appropriate level of emotion.
• Our first strategy: We will consolidate our product lines from 18 to 12. Why? We'll streamline our product lines to 12 for two reasons. First, not all of our products are competitive. Second, our customers say that some lines are simply slow; some lines contain redundant features. So, we've listened and we'll streamline what we sell to our valued customers.	
• Our second strategy: It brings me much grief to announce this next strategy. We have tried to avoid this, but we can no longer ignore reality. Our next strategy is to close our Long Island and Atlanta plants. Yes, we will lose up to 350 people in Long Island and up to 275 in Atlanta. However, I want you to know that we will do everything in our power to offer our friends a wide range of options including geographic transfers, early retirement packages, and job search assistance.	

(continued)

TABLE 7-6 *(continued)*

President's Speech (First Draft)	Why This Is Important
I know our executive team's decisions are difficult for all of us. We will lose trusted and respected colleagues. Yet, if AB Computers is to remain a competitive force, we must follow through on these difficult decisions. It is time for change.	The president must show humanity while moving toward the future and closing the meeting.
I promise you that our executive team will keep you informed every step of the way. Immediately following this session, I ask that you return to your work areas to meet with your managers. Each manager has an information package for you. Your manager will also record your questions and we will give you honest answers on our Intranet.	
And, I ask that you meet with me again in 2 weeks, on the same day of the week, at this same time. I'll share additional information with you then.	
Our Long Island and Atlanta plants participated in meetings this morning and members of our executive team are on site with them throughout the remainder of the week. Rest assured that we will take caring measures to ease this transition for them.	
I sincerely thank you for your time and attention. Remember that it is time for change. And, if we change, then AB Computers can regain its competitive stance in the computer market. Thank you.	

TABLE 7-7   Corporate-wide Communications Work Plan-Draft

Key Events *(Arrange self-stick notes under this column.)*	Timing *(List sequential timing for each key event, by week, under this column. The timeline is up to 6 months; however, a shorter duration for these events is more humane for everyone.)*
Reach consensus at board and executive team meetings regarding severity of problems and necessary next steps.	Finalize during Week 1 (consider this key event as the jumping off point for all other events and communications)
Form a cross-functional communication team (reporting to executive team) responsible for this work plan and all communication events.	Initiate during Week 1
Organize executive team visits to Long Island and Atlanta sites (e.g., for union and plant management discussions, plant closing logistics planning, etc.).	Initiate during Week 1
Hire outplacement firm; work with Legal Department and Human Resources Department to formulate range of opportunities for Long Island and Atlanta site people (e.g., early retirement, transfer opportunities and procedures, job search assistance); document day-of-lay-off procedures for managers, security, HR, Legal Department.	Initiate during Week 2
Hire extra security (e.g., in increasing numbers as lay-off day approaches).	Initiate as needed
Set and communicate procedures to managers regarding handling the media.	Reader: decide timing
Script all news releases.	Reader: decide timing
Script the president's speeches to the organization.	Reader: decide timing
Develop a manager's procedures package to ensure equitable and legal handling of all lay-off situations (e.g., to include policies and procedures, procedural steps to follow, FAQs: frequently asked questions from employees and how to respond to them, etc.).	Reader: decide timing
Create an online question and answer procedure for employees to obtain answers to questions (knowing that some employees are reticent to ask their managers).	Reader: decide timing
Other	Determine as necessary

Case 7-5 Manager on the Defensive

(Case purpose: Coach a manager with interpersonal style issues.)

STEP 1: REVIEW THE BIG PICTURE

In this case, you run a division of 700 people. One of your managers just knocked on your open door: "May I come in and talk to you about something?"

You are busy but you say, "I'm rather busy, Fred. But if it won't take too long, let's talk now."

Fred enters and you join him at your round conference table. (He was promoted into management 2 months ago and you have high hopes for his fast track in the organization.) As Fred shares the following unsettling incident about his interactions with an employee, you realize that Fred's career could be stopped short by his apparent difficulties with anger management.

Fred recounts the situation: "This morning, Sarah came into my office with a complaint. She felt that I'd given a plum assignment to George without asking her if she had room in her schedule to take it on. I explained that George was simply more capable and that I needed someone who wouldn't make any mistakes with this client. You know this client: They bring in 20 percent of our revenues! I just couldn't risk Sarah on this one.

"Anyway, Sarah said that George had five projects at the moment and she only had two. She went on to ask me if gender had anything to do with my decision. I have to admit it: I just blew up. I'm trying to run a department that's suffering from the stiffest competition we've seen in years and she comes in complaining about one measly project assignment. I told her that my decision was final and I also directed her never to question my gender bias again.

"Long story short, she left the office saying that the issue was not settled. By the way, Sarah hasn't been in to see you, has she?"

Your concern grows as Fred explains his conversation with Sarah. You respond by saying, "No, Sarah hasn't been in to see me. However, we need to explore your handling of your conversation with Sarah."

Your task in this case is to:

1. Analyze the risks of Fred's behavior with Sarah.
2. Decide if you should speak with Sarah privately.
3. Coach Fred on how to better handle a situation like this.

STEP 2: ANALYZE FACTS AND EMOTIONS (F&Es)

Ask Fred to Clarify

As Fred's manager, you may not be sure of all the factors that went into Fred's decision to give the project to George as opposed to Sarah. His tenure under you, as a new manager, is relatively short: Thus, you haven't witnessed Fred's managerial style over the long run in a variety of situations. Because of this context, you would do well to check as many facts as you can. You would want to ask Fred a series of questions, such as:

- Could you tell me more about the requirements of this particular client?
- What specific project needs differentiate this client from our other clients?
- I want to have my facts straight: Could you review George's and Sarah's tenures with our company and your department?
- What is the nature and scope of the current projects run by George and Sarah?
- Tell me again: Why is George a better candidate than Sarah to run this project?

Assess Fred's Credibility and Contextual Risk

Fred is a relatively new manager, and his handling of the conversation with Sarah leaves much to be desired. The risks could be high in this situation, especially if Sarah decides to challenge Fred's decision as well as his behavior with her.

However, challenge or no, Fred's behavior should be unacceptable. Why would you view this as a high-risk situation? Take into account the following considerations:

- Fred apparently did little to demonstrate to Sarah that he heard, and understood *her* concerns.
- Fred lost his temper when challenged by his employee. This is not a good sign: What might Fred do in another similar situation or one that requires him to remain calm under greater fire?
- Fred minimized Sarah's concerns by telling her never to bring up the question of gender bias again. His overreaction might only fuel Sarah's suspicions.
- Sarah may discuss the interaction with Fred among her colleagues, thus endangering this new manager's credibility with others.

Coach Fred

You must make time to coach Fred, whether you think you have time or not. If you can only fit a brief discussion in at this time, schedule an additional session in the near future.

Fred's answers to your probing questions (see the previous list) will give you important information about how Fred approaches and solves problems. The nature of your coaching session will, of course, depend on how Fred responds to you. However, at least help Fred envision and comprehend why his behavior with Sarah could create unnecessary problems (see "Step 3: Design the Strategy").

Decide if you Should Speak with Sarah Privately

This decision depends on your organizational culture, your managerial style, and the extent to which you trust Fred to handle the damage control without you. Your decision also depends on Sarah's behavior on the job and how you think she might react. There is no clear-cut answer; however, the answer should result from your conversation with Fred, and you should include Fred in the decision. You do not want to usurp Fred's authority yet—unless there is a real reason to do so.

STEP 3: DESIGN THE STRATEGY

Your coaching session(s) with Fred should, at the least, cover the following:

- State the risks that Fred's behavior might incur for him, you, and the company.

- Explain how Fred's perceptions, reactions, and responses might differ from yours. Perhaps share a couple of anecdotal stories with Fred to illuminate the potential consequences of such managerial behavior.
- Ask Fred to walk you through a hypothetical conversation with Sarah—to illustrate how he would better handle the situation. You cannot do the talking here: Let Fred talk so that you can identify the flawed points in his reactions and problem solving.
- Walk Fred through how you might have handled the conversation with Sarah and why. Fred must begin to see that there are alternate, and more suitable, emotional reactions.
- Ask Fred to walk you through a second conversation with Sarah: because you will require him to talk with Sarah again and attempt to clarify the situation (without anger). Again, listen, and coach Fred on any points that could be improved.
- If you feel that Fred is not ready for a private discussion with Sarah, state that you and Fred will meet with Sarah as soon as possible.
- Ask Fred questions such as: What really bothers you about all this? Do my ideas make sense to you? What might you add to the approach we've just discussed?

Case 7-6 Employee Blow-Up
(Case purpose: Manage an employee's display of anger during a meeting.)

STEP 1: REVIEW THE BIG PICTURE

Assume that you manage a group of 15 professional and technical experts. You are conducting a biweekly departmental meeting in your small conference room. The discussion becomes rather heated as your group discusses how to streamline intra-departmental communications regarding client projects. Current procedures require people to write a status report of approximately two pages and copy everyone in the department. Most people believe that everyone needs the information because so many of your department's experts come in and out of projects on an as-needed basis.

As the discussion progresses, one person becomes increasingly agitated: We'll call this person Lee (you select the gender for the purposes of this case). Everyone, except Lee, agrees that a streamlined status report could be created using a table format. One person in the group, Mary, just moments ago sketched a few ideas on a flip chart. The conversation proceeds as follows:

MARY: "See, if we use a table format instead of a paragraph-based format, we'll save a lot of writing time if—"

LEE: (interrupting) "We all need the details. How can we know what's really happening if we don't see all the details?"

MARY: "We'll still have the details. See, the headings could reflect all the critical pieces of information that we need—"

LEE: (interrupting again and tightly grasping the table) "I don't buy it. You can't sell me on this idea. As soon as client questions come up, we'll all be scrambling around looking for answers."

CLARISSE: (a technical expert) "But, Lee, I like the idea. It isn't as hard as it seems. Why don't we just test it and see if it is easier?"

Everyone nods, and several people say, "Yeah, let's try it."

LEE: (voice has raised considerably in volume) "Why don't we get someone in here that knows something about project management! Here we all sit, yapping and drawing pictures like a bunch of grade-school kids. And we don't know what we're doing. The idea is stupid. No way."

At this point, everyone in the meeting sits quiet; seemingly, no one knows how to respond to Lee.

Your task is to decide whether or not to intervene at this point in the discussion. If you intervene, what will you do?

STEP 2: ANALYZE FACTS AND EMOTIONS (F&Es)

A manager in this situation would certainly have to consider the context when deciding how to communicate with Lee and the group. The manager would rapidly think through a range of questions before deciding how to respond: This requires fast thinking and intuitive reasoning. For example:

- What is the perceived risk that Lee's anger might escalate into threatening or dangerous behavior?
- What kind of informal power base does Lee hold among group members?
- Is the altercation between Lee and Mary (and later Clarisse) representative of some power play or long-standing rift?
- What meaning would people attribute to manager intervention at this point?
- Is conflict an acceptable part of this group's culture?
- What is the risk that this conflict, if allowed to escalate, might result in a serious wedge through the group?
- Does Lee often react in this manner?
- Is the manager aware of any difficult issues in Lee's life, unrelated to the question at hand?
- If the manager waits for the people to resolve the conflict, would employees question the manager's ability as a leader?
- Is there a simple cause for Lee's behavior? For example, is Lee threatened because she or he does not know how to work in tables on the computer?

The answers to these questions would lead the manager to a decision. Yes, I'll intervene; no, I won't intervene. Let's assume that the manager decides to intervene. Now the manager must decide whether to take a strong stand or to divert Lee's anger in a less straightforward way. The manager quickly envisions a range of scenarios:

- If the manager confronts Lee, then Lee might react with more anger. Why? Because Lee, in effect, is given no way out. Lee is backed into a corner in front of a group of people, and a person in anger usually responds with more anger when confronted.
- If the manager and Lee engage in a head to head disagreement, then a battle for power (in front of all onlookers) could result. Is there a winner in this scenario? No, the group grows increasingly uncomfortable as they watch a colleague and their manager vie for power.
- If the manager diverts Lee's and the group's attention for a time, then Lee's anger might dissipate. This strategy allows Lee to save face without winning or losing.
- If the manager allows Lee to continue his or her negative behavior, then the group might react negatively. Once an entire group focuses on the negative, then any creative flow is lost.

STEP 3: DESIGN THE STRATEGY

For the purposes of discussion, let's select the following managerial response: If the manager diverts Lee's and the group's attention for a time, then potentially Lee's anger might dissipate. This strategy allows Lee to save face without winning or losing.

Depending on the assumptions you made (e.g., could Lee become violent, would Lee's comments insert a serious wedge through the group), you would respond accordingly. For example, if the risk of Lee becoming violent were high, the manager would certainly quickly intervene. The manager would want to put physical space between Lee and others in the group. The manager could, in a worst case scenario, need to request assistance from security.

But let's assume that a simple intervention would work. The manager does not have to take over the meeting. The manager could simply divert attention, and minimize tension, by saying something like the following: "Let me ask a question here. Mary, do you know how to create such a table? (Assume that Mary says yes.) Well, I want to give this more thought. Please send this week's status report to all of us in table format. Everyone else, please write your status reports as you've always done: in paragraph form. I want to see the two formats, and I ask that everyone review the two formats and refer to them as needed during your usual project work. Let's defer a decision until we can at least see what Mary is talking about. We'll continue to talk about this at our next meeting. (Pause.) You know, perhaps the table format makes sense for some of us, but not the whole group. Or, over time, we may see a need to change. Let's wait and see."

What works with this diversion strategy? What might not work? What would you do differently?

Case 7-7 Freelance Delegation Dilemma

(Case purpose: Manage a difficult freelance situation in a tight turnaround.)

STEP 1: REVIEW THE BIG PICTURE

You, within the parameters of this case, are a project manager on an international, high-visibility project. Eleven people comprise your staff team. In addition, you hired two free-lancers to write a series of deliverables for this large project: employee communication updates (for delivery via e-mail), and direct line supervisor and manager hands-on materials (for management to use when motivating people and gaining their buy-in on this project).

One of the freelance writers produces quality documents that match your instructions; the second freelance writer delivers quality documents that don't match stated expectations. You've spent a good amount of time with both people and you feel that you've given them an equitable level of instructions.

However, when you confront the second freelance writer, the writer responds by saying that your instructions were vague and that the writer didn't fully understand what you wanted. During your conversation, it becomes clear that it is a "he said, she said" dilemma: You have no copies of the notes to the writer and you did not maintain a file of when and how instructions were given.

Your task is to decide your options, ranging from (a) removing this freelance writer from the assignment to (b) keeping this writer but closely monitoring all assignments. You face a difficult deadline, however; all documents must be completed, edited, and sent to the client in 7 days. You probably cannot bring a new writer up to speed and the first writer cannot take on additional work.

STEPS 2 AND 3: ANALYZE FACTS AND EMOTIONS (F&Es) AND DESIGN THE STRATEGY

Factually speaking, you have a range of options. The emotional costs inherent in some of those options, after consideration, should preclude you from selecting all but one of them.

You could terminate the freelancer's project contract. However, then you would have no good place to go with the work. If you ask the other freelancer or your staff to take on the workload, you would probably meet with frustration and perhaps resistance. Your communication task, with this option, could prove overwhelming.

You could take on the work yourself. This is, to say the least, a poor alternative. The implied message communicated to the team by this action is not a good one: You, as leader, must remain actively in a true leadership role to bring this project successfully to completion.

You could pair the freelance writer with a project team member. Your communication task would be to convince the team member to take on the additional supervisory responsibilities required by the freelancer. You would have to carefully select the team member because of the additional workload and potential frustrations posed by the freelancer's behaviors. You face the communication challenge of convincing the team member of the *overarching value* of this additional work (e.g., value to the client, the project, and the company and team's reputation). You must also convince the team member of the potential *personal value* (e.g., benefits such as special notation on performance review, compensation time, public thanks in project team meetings; the list is only limited by your imagination and what is appropriate to the context).

Case 7-8 Perception Dilemma (Sharing Perceived as Losing)
(Case purpose: Use customer perceptions to cause internal improvements.)

STEP 1: REVIEW THE BIG PICTURE

You are, during this case, the leader of a company that employs 3,000 people. You have the typical functional *silos* in your organization: marketing, operations, sales, finance, etc. Today you sit at a conference table with your division heads; your purpose is to explore how to enhance interdepartmental communications and thus increase customer satisfaction.

The real need for this focus came from two sources:

- Customer satisfaction survey results: Customers, in essence, complain that the advertising promises don't match the services sold and delivered.
- Employee satisfaction survey results: Employees, all too often, complain that the departments don't keep the other groups informed and that "we look ill-informed in front of our clients."

Your organization has been slow to embrace these issues: This is the third round of annual customer and employee satisfaction surveys highlighting the problem. However, customer complaints have increased, your market share has dropped, and your employee turnover is the highest ever. The management team has heard countless anecdotal comments from different people in various divisions and departments about the same mistakes being made with clients.

You've finally convinced the management team to stop worrying about the symptoms and to begin finding real solutions to the root cause: Your people believe that *sharing means losing*. Your people are afraid to say, "Hey, we made a mistake on this project. Let me tell you how not to make the same mistake." You and your managers, after conducting several focus groups about the issues, believe that it is finally time to act.

Your task is to brainstorm the following problem statement: "How can we support and promote internal behaviors that *equate sharing with winning* for everyone?" This case requires that readers simulate a brainstorm session (see the Appendix to Chapter 3: "Review of Facilitation Tools").

STEP 2: ANALYZE FACTS AND EMOTIONS (F&Es)

People fear change and individuals fear looking bad in front of others. A key element of conducting this brainstorm is to first create a *safe* environment for participants. People invited to the brainstorm must be told, from the beginning, that all ideas are anonymous and that no one will be blamed for any comments.

The facilitator might briefly discuss similar problems in another company and describe how the people in that organization rallied together to find new answers. Finally, the facilitator would have to be empowered to tell participants that management will, in fact, follow through on changes and positive steps. (You would not want people to think that they're sharing ideas, once again, while management will do nothing to help change the situation.)

STEP 3: DESIGN THE STRATEGY

An effective strategy might follow these talking and meeting facilitation points:

1. Welcome and introduce participants
2. State purpose of brainstorm and explain the problem statement (answer any questions about the problem statement in 5 minutes or less)
3. Describe how another organization experienced and solved a similar problem
4. Describe the 1.5-hour time limit for the brainstorm
5. Review brainstorm guidelines (e.g., no bad ideas, no criticism, state the idea or comment simply in about 12 words)
6. Explain the brainstorm methodology to be used today
7. Initiate the brainstorm
8. Conduct the brainstorm
9. Review the results (e.g., ideas and comments)
10. Explain next steps
11. Thank participants

How might you facilitate this brainstorm differently?

Bibliography

Cooper, R. K., and Sawaf, A. (1997). *Executive EQ: Emotional Intelligence in Leadership and Organizations*. New York: The Berkley Publishing Group.

Fisher, A. (1998). Success secret: A high emotional IQ. *Fortune*, October 26.

Haden Elgin, S. (1989). *The Gentle Art of Verbal Self-Defense for Business Success*. Upper Saddle River, NJ: Prentice Hall.

Howard, C. M., and Mathews, W. K. (2000). *On Deadline: Managing Media Relations* (3rd Ed.). Prospect Heights, IL: Waveland Press, Inc.

Index